THE TELLING ROOM PRESENTS

# THE STORY I WANT TO TELL

EXPLORATIONS IN THE ART OF WRITING

Tilbury House, Publishers
Thomaston, Maine

*The Story I Want to Tell*
Copyright © 2014 The Telling Room
Paperback ISBN 978-0-88448-415-8
eBook ISBN 978-0-88448-422-6

Cover design by Might & Main, Portland, ME
Text design by Janet Robbins, North Wind Publishing & Design, Brewer, ME

Concept by Molly McGrath & Ari Meil
Edited by Molly McGrath with Erin Bartnett, David Caron, Abigail Chance, Susan Conley, Gibson Fay-LeBlanc, Andrew Griswold, and Rose Heithoff

"Burning in the Rain" is from *Looking for The Gulf Motel*, by Richard Blanco, © 2012. Reprinted by permission of the University of Pittsburgh Press. "Go to Jail, After Eight Times, Go Directly to Jail" is excerpted from "The Great Divider" in *Braindead Megaphone*. Reprinted by permission of Riverhead Books, an imprint of Penguin Group (USA) Inc. "Pull the Sled, Feed the Fire" appeared originally in *Smith Journal* magazine: smithjournal.com.au

*Library of Congress Cataloging-in-Publication Data*

The Story I Want to Tell : Explorations in the Art of Writing.
     pages         cm
  At head of title : The Telling Room Presents
  ISBN 978-0-88448-415-8
  1. American literature—21st century. 2. Authorship. I. Telling Room. II. Title:
The Telling Room Presents.
  PS536.3.S76 2014
  810.8'006—dc23          2014031594

Printed in the United States of America

14 15 16 17 18 19 MAP 10 9 8 7 6 5 4 3 2 1

Scan this code to go to the Tilbury House website for more about this book.

# THE STORY I WANT TO TELL

# CONTENTS

## INTERVIEWS WITH THE WRITERS

# INTRODUCTION

The word "inspire" comes from the Latin for *enflame* or *to fill the mind, heart, or soul with grace, with the breath of something otherworldly.* This book's title was inspired by a high school student's excitement as he sat with his writing mentor on the cold floor of a hallway outside his alternative education classroom and began to narrate "the story I want to tell." It was the one in his pocket, the one in his heart, the one he possessed and that possessed him. The one that inspired him.

Whether or not you've killed a hyena, turned into a carrot, run from a giant alligator, imagined a sandwich grinning, floated an origami box in a distant ocean, or watched a dragonfly devour its prey, the stories and poems in this book will take you across time and place. They put you on the spot. And maybe they'll inspire you to tell your own story.

## The Story of the Book

The Telling Room is a nonprofit writing center in downtown Portland, Maine—a big sunny loft where thousands of kids come every year to watch their stories grow. During its first ten years, The Telling Room has worked with more than 10,000 young writers and printed their work in nearly fifty publications. Telling Room kids write the kinds of stories that grab you and don't let go.

This book is a celebration of The Telling Room's first ten years and its enduring belief in the power of storytelling. To mark this milestone, we knew we wanted to make a special book, a "best of," and so we selected twenty of the best pieces from those thousands of young writers—a daunting task—and paired them with brand-new answering pieces from award-winning writers. We thought a lot about how to match our student storytellers with these acclaimed authors who supported them and The Telling Room so well over our first decade. Sometimes the matchmaking was easy, even uncannily so, but never was the responding author's task an easy one. Answering such charged poems and powerful stories took guts and heart.

One of the main goals of this book is connection—breaking down the barriers of age and experience. The young authors have truly leveled the playing field, and many of the adult writers felt humbled when trying to match the intensity of emotion many of the kids' stories elicit. One adult author wrote and edited a complete draft many times over before rejecting it because it just wasn't coming out right. We gave him another student's piece, and this one clicked. He remarked that this second piece gave him permission and the inspiration he needed to write a story he'd long wanted to tell about his grandfather in Thailand. A connection was born, as happened time and again through these pairs of writing, and in this way the book came together.

So there you have it. *The Story I Want to Tell* is a compilation of forty stories, essays, and poems told in pairs. It pays tribute to newly discovered writers and to masters of the craft. All have been published before. Some have achieved worldwide fame, and many are rising stars. In the end, what happens here is more than we could have hoped for. It is a conversation in words between young and adult writers. The "call and response" pieces talk to each other in mysterious, transcendent ways—echoing themes, reinventing characters, retracing plot lines. They talk to the other pairings and to readers, too. They can be read cover to cover or by mood, theme, subject, or genre. The conversation gets richer in the interviews after the pairings and in the writing prompts at the end of the book, and we hope continues further with the stories you want to tell.

## About the Contributors

All the storytellers between these covers know The Telling Room well. The kids here participated in Telling Room programs, and their pieces were previously published in our annual anthologies. In our first ten years, celebrated authors Elizabeth Gilbert, George Saunders, Dave Eggers, Ann Beattie, Campbell McGrath, and Jonathan Lethem held intimate roundtable conversations with groups of Telling Room students and gave standing-room-only community readings. Bill Roorbach, Richard Russo, Betsy Sholl, and Richard Blanco are part of an esteemed Telling Room author committee. Ari Meil, Lily King, Melissa Coleman, Jaed Coffin, and Gibson Fay-LeBlanc have served as Telling Room staff and board members and have conducted workshops alongside Robinson and Wood. The Telling Room's founders—Susan Conley, Sara Corbett, and Mike Paterniti—have worked with our kids since the beginning and are here as well. Sara and Mike have special relationships with the authors to whom they chose to respond, having served as their writing mentors in The Telling Room's first funded program.

It may be that you found this book because of the famous names in the table of contents, but once you read through the entire collection, we bet you'll realize something that we discovered at The Telling Room years ago: Children are the most amazing natural storytellers. Their stories, whether prose or verse, are raw, startling, and truthful, because a young person's greatest wish is often just to tell a story straight. Kids don't yet have the conceit to tell it otherwise, and therein lies their power. And the juxtaposition of the contributors—young and old—tells its own story. That the esteemed, widely published authors in this book not only read the young writers' pieces but also were inspired to write their own sends a powerful message: Adults are not the only source of inspiration, creativity, and knowledge. These things are in all of us. We all have stories we want to tell, and we all can write and share them.

— MOLLY McGRATH
The Telling Room

# A NOTE FOR WRITING INSTRUCTORS

There are many tools for teachers in this book. Following the paired writings is a section of candid interviews with the contributors about their writing lives, the writing process, and the publishing process. A host of writing prompts appears in the back of the book and is also available to print online at: www.tellingroom.org/thestoryiwanttotell. These prompts may be useful as topics for classroom discussion and for out-of-classroom exploration as well. In a broader sense, of course, every selection in this book is a writing prompt. That is, any story or poem that moves you and inspires you to feel differently is a blueprint for how to write.

This book can be used as a core text in a writing classroom, a literary anthology for outside reading, or a book club selection. Teachers can use it to show students that their voices are valuable and powerful and that their stories are not only worth telling but quite possibly worthy of being published and shared widely. Students can read the work of other students and adults, deriving inspiration for their own writing from the diverse range of ideas, themes, styles, and voices here.

*The Story I Want to Tell* is meant for reluctant and already flourishing writing students. Through our decade of working with students at The Telling Room, we have seen that when students read their peers' writing in our books, they are transformed from resistant to inspired writers themselves. They experience an increased sense of creativity and self-confidence when they realize that kids like themselves have been published, and that by modeling their peers' work, they can write and share their writing, too. When they finish reading stories—often about ordinary things or relatable people, places, or situations—some of the most hesitant think, "Oh, I can tell that story!" And once they set to it, they realize what was inside them all along.

We believe that these examples of good writing will help young writers develop their storytelling and writing skills and make their voices heard. Maybe—like the thousands of Telling Room kids before them—they will be stimulated to write their own pieces, start a writing club, publish their own magazine, or read their writing for an audience at an open mic or their book release party. They should have a chance to find out firsthand that people want to hear their stories. We hope this book helps give them that chance.

ALI MOHAMED, Hyenas
ELIZABETH GILBERT, Cheekbone

AMIRA AL SAMMRAI, Breathing in the Rain
RICHARD BLANCO, Burning in the Rain

CHRISTINA MURRAY, Carrots
JONATHAN LETHEM, Carrot-Spotting

COLIN SHEPARD, Wildernesses
BILL ROORBACH, Heat Rises

ELIAS NASRAT, The Fate of the Trees
BETSY SHOLL, That Leafless Tree

HASSAN JEYLANI, A Day in Three Worlds
CAMPBELL MCGRATH, Night and Day

JULIAN MAYORQUIN, Bottle Jacking
GEORGE SAUNDERS, Go to Jail, After Eight Times, Go Directly to Jail

RICHARD AKERA, I Started to Explain
RICHARD RUSSO, Drinking Water

VASSILY MURANGIRA, Swimming to Safety
ANN BEATTIE, Drive-by Alligator

JANET MATHIESON, A Sandwich/An Olive
ARI MEIL, Jammy Brightness

MAHAD HILOWLE, The Table
SUSAN CONLEY, The Table

DARCIE SERFES, The Bump
LILY KING, Summer

NOAH WILLIAMS, Hunting in the Deep Woods
LEWIS ROBINSON, When Dad Rode Past Me

MICHÉE RUNYAMBO, Two Teeth
MONICA WOOD, History Lesson

EMILY HOLLYDAY, Cantaloupe
GIBSON FAY-LEBLANC, Self-Portrait, with Dish Rag

MISSOURI ALICE WILLIAMS, A Little Secret
MELISSA COLEMAN, Goddess of Liberation

FADUMO ISSACK, Climbing Barefoot
JAED COFFIN, The Coconut Tree

GRACE WHITED, Box of Hope
DAVE EGGERS, Pull the Sled, Feed the Fire

AQILA SHARAFYAR, The Faithful Doves of My Father
SARA CORBETT, I Thought I Could Fix Things

ARUNA KENYI, The Photograph
MICHAEL PATERNITI, We Are Trying to Understand What Happened to You There

# Hyenas

*ALI MOHAMED*

My grandmother always told me that I should be afraid of the lions, but not to be afraid of the hyenas. My grandmother lived in our village and helped my mother cook. She died before my father died, but I remember the stories that she told me. She said that you should never run away from a hyena because they will kill you, but if you don't run away, they will not kill you. My brothers and sisters were afraid of hyenas, but not me. They had seen a hyena eat something down by the river once, and it scared them.

At night, we put our goats inside the fence that went around the house. One morning, a hyena jumped the fence, grabbed a goat by its neck, and jumped back out of the fence. My father said to me, "Wake up! Go get that hyena who stole our goat!" So I ran after him. I hid behind a tree and when the hyena went by, I hit his kidneys with a club and he fell down. My grandmother had told me not to bother hitting them in the head. You can hit them all day in the head and nothing will happen, but if you hit them in the kidneys they will die, she said. My father ran over to me with a knife, and he gave the knife to me. He was afraid of the hyena. Then my father said, "Kill him!" I stabbed the knife into the hyena's stomach. That was the first time I killed a hyena. It was before my father died, and he died when I was five years old.

After that all the people in the village came to me and said, "Oh, you killed a hyena!" My grandmother had told me not to be afraid of hyenas and I wasn't afraid. When you are small like that, the big people think it is funny that you are not afraid—they think you are brave. My father was proud of me, too.

My father was a kind man, and he was very tall—he was maybe ten or eleven feet tall! Well, I don't know how tall he was; I never asked him, "How tall are you, Father?" But when we walked together, while going to the ocean or to town, and he held my hand, I looked way up into the sky to see him. My mother says I am getting tall like my father.

There was a village in Somalia where I lived, when I was five, with my mother, father, my two brothers, and my sister. There were maybe twenty-five farms in this village. We had a round house made of wood. Inside the house were two beds where we slept. There was one bed for my parents, one bed for my sister, and my brothers and I slept on the floor between them. Every day it took hours for my father to walk back and forth from the store he owned in a town nearby, where he sold food and soap and things like that. He would leave at six in the morning, and he would return at six at night. Sometimes, my mother would send me to bring him his lunch, and I would walk there and back all by myself. Sometimes, I would return on a different road because I liked to go through the forest, but my parents told me not to go on that road because they thought I might get lost, or there might be animals in the forest. But I never got lost, nor did I ever see any animals in the forest to be afraid of.

Nothing had ever happened in my village. It was a very quiet village. I don't think that anyone had ever been killed there before. It was a Sunday night. I remember everything about that night. It was in the summer of 1992. It was 12:30 A.M. We were all awake. There were men with big guns who surrounded our house. They looked like they were in the army. My mother said that we were the minority tribe, and they were fighting against us and that is why they were there. Or maybe they had seen my father coming from his store in the town and thought that my father had a lot of money.

One of them had a chopped-off arm; there was no hand below his elbow. He seemed to be the commander, and he was the worst of them. He told everyone to come out of the house and to lie down on the ground. He said, "Where is the father of this house?" My little three-year-old-brother told them that my father was in the outhouse. Then the commander without a hand, without saying anything, shot him. Just like that, without thinking, he just shot him, and he died. The soldiers went to the outhouse and kicked down the door. The outhouse was up on the rocks, and there was no way he could have escaped from it.

The commander with the chopped-off arm told my father to come out, and when he did, the commander then told him to get on the ground. Nobody was moving. A few minutes later, the commander said to one of the soldiers, "Why are you looking at that man? Kill him!" Then they shot my father. He died. My mother screamed, "Why did you kill him?" The soldiers asked the commander if they should shoot her. The commander didn't care about anything and he said, "Look at her!" and then he shot her. The shot hit her leg. She was alive, but badly injured.

They took everything we had. They took my father's store money, my mother's earrings, and anything good we had. Then they left, and people from the village came. A friend and my older brother, who was ten at the time, took my mother away in a cart pulled by a donkey to get her to someone who could help the wound in her leg. I tried to follow them but they told me to stay in the village. Some other villagers buried my father and my little brother.

When my brother got my mother to the doctor, they told him that there was nothing they could do for her. It was not a place where they could do surgery. My uncle gave someone some money so that she could go the hospital in Kenya. My uncle, my brother, and my father's friend all took her there, and she was in the hospital in Kenya for two or three years. I missed my mother for those long years. I lived with my sister in the village. She made cakes that we brought to the town to sell.

When my mother came back to Somalia to get me, my sister decided to move to another village, and we never saw her again. She got married and she has two children. My mother, my brother, and I moved to the Hagadera, a refugee camp in Kenya. We lived there for two years. I liked it there. I had lots of friends, we played soccer, I went to school and learned English. I had a girlfriend there; she is still there, and I still talk to her on the phone sometimes.

One time, my friends at the refugee camp and I were talking, and they said they didn't believe that I had killed a hyena. They were afraid of the hyenas. I told them to ask my mother if I had killed a hyena in my village. Then one morning, early, they took me over to the slaughterhouse where there were always hyenas lurking around. I told them to give me a club. I started running towards some hyenas, there were three or four together and then I dove on to the ground and grabbed the legs of one of the hyenas, then I hit him in the kidneys, like my grandmother had told me to. That's how I killed that hyena. Then I took a rope and I tied his legs together. My friends said, "This is amazing that you can kill hyenas like that!" Then they said, "Every Friday we will come here, and you will kill a hyena." But I said, "No."

I was fourteen when I killed that hyena and I lived in the refugee camp in Kenya. Now I am seventeen and I live on Merrill Street in Portland, Maine. It is peaceful here, except sometimes in my dreams. Coming to America has meant going back, again and again in my mind, to these stories I am telling. My mother wants me to forget, but I cannot. I would like someday to go back to

Kenya, perhaps go to the university there. And I would like to ask my girlfriend there to marry me.

But I'm done killing hyenas. At least I hope so. I'm almost as tall as my father now, and I've nothing left to prove.

# Cheekbone

*Elizabeth Gilbert*

The thing is, have you ever seen a hyena?

More to the point, have you ever seen a hyena's jaw? I saw one once, when I was in college, taking a zoology class. We were comparing the jaws of carnivores, one against another, and somebody put a hyena's skull into my hands. It was terrifying. This was the lifeless, odorless, ivory-colored, smooth and harmless skull of a long-dead animal, and still, it was terrifying. It wasn't the fangs that got me (all carnivores have fangs); it was the dramatic shape of the zygomatic arch.

You probably know the zygomatic arch by its more common name—the cheekbone. In the anatomy of all of us, the tendons and muscles required for biting pass through and beside this critical little bone. In hyenas, however, the jaw muscles are so huge that the arch itself is rather shockingly enormous, in order to accommodate this incredible bulk of musculature. Such ingenious architecture creates a bite force in hyenas that is about forty percent more powerful than that of your friendly neighborhood leopard. A hyena can kill a large dog in one bite, without even breaking the skin of the neck. A hyena can shatter the femur of a giraffe in a matter of moments. It can eat through an elephant's leg.

So the image of tiny Ali Mohamed chasing after a hyena with nothing more than a club and his father's knife sent a chill through me. A five-year-old human child has no business messing around with an animal like this. No matter what his grandmother may say.

But the real power of this story, which set in long after the soul-shifting image of that hyena skull again in my hand, comes in the gradual realization that hyenas are the least of Ali's concerns. It's the men with guns who come in the night that he had to worry about. The sort of men who murder people's fathers. The men who might shoot his three-year-old brother for no discernible reason whatsoever. The men who might maim his mother and (this is a particularly heartbreaking tiny human detail) steal her earrings.

Then comes the refugee camp. Then comes the dislocation to a new and snow-covered world. Then come the dreams that do not ever pass.

How can anyone endure all this? Especially such a young person? By becoming taller than your own father, it seems. By remembering who you are. Somebody who has already proven so much in the way of his own courage that he has nothing left to kill or fight. Ali Mohamed does not make survival look easy, but he does make it look possible.

Back to anatomy, in conclusion: The hyena also has a disproportionately large heart—double the size, relatively speaking, of a lion's heart. This adaptation gives the creature stupendous, almost impossible to imagine powers of endurance.

Some people are like that, too.

ALI MOHAMED, Hyenas
ELIZABETH GILBERT, Cheekbone

**AMIRA AL SAMMRAI, Breathing in the Rain**
**RICHARD BLANCO, Burning in the Rain**

CHRISTINA MURRAY, Carrots
JONATHAN LETHEM, Carrot-Spotting

COLIN SHEPARD, Wildernesses
BILL ROORBACH, Heat Rises

ELIAS NASRAT, The Fate of the Trees
BETSY SHOLL, That Leafless Tree

HASSAN JEYLANI, A Day in Three Worlds
CAMPBELL MCGRATH, Night and Day

JULIAN MAYORQUIN, Bottle Jacking
GEORGE SAUNDERS, Go to Jail, After Eight Times, Go Directly to Jail

RICHARD AKERA, I Started to Explain
RICHARD RUSSO, Drinking Water

VASSILY MURANGIRA, Swimming to Safety
ANN BEATTIE, Drive-by Alligator

JANET MATHIESON, A Sandwich/An Olive
ARI MEIL, Jammy Brightness

MAHAD HILOWLE, The Table
SUSAN CONLEY, The Table

DARCIE SERFES, The Bump
LILY KING, Summer

NOAH WILLIAMS, Hunting in the Deep Woods
LEWIS ROBINSON, When Dad Rode Past Me

MICHÉE RUNYAMBO, Two Teeth
MONICA WOOD, History Lesson

EMILY HOLLYDAY, Cantaloupe
GIBSON FAY-LEBLANC, Self-Portrait, with Dish Rag

MISSOURI ALICE WILLIAMS, A Little Secret
MELISSA COLEMAN, Goddess of Liberation

FADUMO ISSACK, Climbing Barefoot
JAED COFFIN, The Coconut Tree

GRACE WHITED, Box of Hope
DAVE EGGERS, Pull the Sled, Feed the Fire

AQILA SHARAFYAR, The Faithful Doves of My Father
SARA CORBETT, I Thought I Could Fix Things

ARUNA KENYI, The Photograph
MICHAEL PATERNITI, We Are Trying to Understand What Happened to You There

# Breathing in the Rain

*Amira Al Sammrai*

One time I lived
In a room with a window
I had to lean far out of
To see a small patch of sky.
I could hear the children playing outside
But through that window I saw
No sunlight and no stars.
I couldn't tell if it was day or night.
I was in a small bird's cage.

I remember one night
The clouds hugged each other
And the sky rained.
That night I hated to stay
In my room so I went out
To breathe the roses' perfume
And see rain falling on the paper bark
Of trees washed from the hot season.
Thin water flowed between my feet.

Back inside the rain fell on my window
Making a beautiful voice
And mixing its steam with my breath.
That day I flew with the raindrops
And I saw the gardens and deserts.
I saw farms, I saw houses.
The rain is a miracle of god.
After the rain eased
I could still smell it
And I went to bed
To sleep and to wash my heart again.

# Burning in the Rain

*Richard Blanco*

Someday compassion would demand
I set myself free of my desire to recreate
my father, indulge in my mother's losses,
strangle lovers with words, forcing them
to confess for me and take the blame.
Today was that day: I tossed them, sheet
by sheet on the patio and gathered them
into a pyre. I wanted to let them go
in a blaze, tiny white dwarfs imploding
beside the azaleas and ficus bushes,
let them crackle, burst like winged seeds,
let them smolder into gossamer embers—
a thousand gray butterflies in the wind.
Today was that day, but it rained, kept
raining. Instead of fire, water—drops
knocking on doors, wetting windows
into mirrors reflecting me in the oaks.
The garden walls and stones swelling
into ghostlier shades of themselves,
the wind chimes giggling in the storm,
a coffee cup left overflowing with rain.
Instead of burning, my pages turned
into water lilies floating over puddles,
then tiny white cliffs as the sun set,
finally drying all night under the moon
into papier-mâché souvenirs. Today
the rain would not let their lives burn.

ALI MOHAMED, Hyenas
ELIZABETH GILBERT, Cheekbone

AMIRA AL SAMMRAI, Breathing in the Rain
RICHARD BLANCO, Burning in the Rain

**CHRISTINA MURRAY, Carrots**
**JONATHAN LETHEM, Carrot-Spotting**

COLIN SHEPARD, Wildernesses
BILL ROORBACH, Heat Rises

ELIAS NASRAT, The Fate of the Trees
BETSY SHOLL, That Leafless Tree

HASSAN JEYLANI, A Day in Three Worlds
CAMPBELL MCGRATH, Night and Day

JULIAN MAYORQUIN, Bottle Jacking
GEORGE SAUNDERS, Go to Jail, After Eight Times, Go Directly to Jail

RICHARD AKERA, I Started to Explain
RICHARD RUSSO, Drinking Water

VASSILY MURANGIRA, Swimming to Safety
ANN BEATTIE, Drive-by Alligator

JANET MATHIESON, A Sandwich/An Olive
ARI MEIL, Jammy Brightness

MAHAD HILOWLE, The Table
SUSAN CONLEY, The Table

DARCIE SERFES, The Bump
LILY KING, Summer

NOAH WILLIAMS, Hunting in the Deep Woods
LEWIS ROBINSON, When Dad Rode Past Me

MICHÉE RUNYAMBO, Two Teeth
MONICA WOOD, History Lesson

EMILY HOLLYDAY, Cantaloupe
GIBSON FAY-LEBLANC, Self-Portrait, with Dish Rag

MISSOURI ALICE WILLIAMS, A Little Secret
MELISSA COLEMAN, Goddess of Liberation

FADUMO ISSACK, Climbing Barefoot
JAED COFFIN, The Coconut Tree

GRACE WHITED, Box of Hope
DAVE EGGERS, Pull the Sled, Feed the Fire

AQILA SHARAFYAR, The Faithful Doves of My Father
SARA CORBETT, I Thought I Could Fix Things

ARUNA KENYI, The Photograph
MICHAEL PATERNITI, We Are Trying to Understand What Happened to You There

# Carrots

*Christina Murray*

When I was nine, I wished I could be a carrot. I would have gotten to disappear behind a cliff of meatloaf or under a river of gravy at the dinner table. I would've been able to travel, too, even if it meant only in the back of Mr. Gripes's beat-up farm pickup that chugged past me to distant market places as I walked home from school.

If I had been a carrot, I wouldn't have had to hear Mama crying about losing another one of her sons. I wouldn't have had to hear Daddy when he came home, a strange smell drifting from his lips, yelling at Joey and me about the undercooked sausage that we had made because our mother was too depressed to leave her bed. That bed held her like a tree branch grasping an apple stem. I didn't want to be an apple, though. I always wanted to be a carrot.

It wouldn't have been difficult for me to become a carrot; all the kids at school already called me Carrot Top. My eyes matched the leaves sprouting from the head of the vegetable. I don't think I would have been the only carrot; I knew Joey would have wanted to be one, too, and maybe even John, if he weren't too caught up in whatever girl sat next to him on our spinach-colored couch. And certainly Mama; she would've wanted to be a carrot. It wouldn't have been any problem for them either, because they also had red hair.

If I had been a carrot, I know I would have been normal. I wouldn't have been the fourth grader who sat in silence, afraid to slip up and tell her secret. But I knew that if I said one word that hinted at the bruises that lived on my arm like the black spots on an old banana's skin, then another eggplant-colored blotch would join them. Ah, but if I had been a carrot, I would have had real friends, made of tomato-colored blood and bones the shade of cauliflower, instead of the nonexistent people who lived only in my head.

Even when I was seventeen I wanted to be a carrot. I longed to live underground with Hades and Persephone, the tragic heroine I read about at the lunch table in the lemony cafeteria. I wanted so much to live with Mama and Joey again, but they had been crushed like a crabapple under the hoof of a horse when they drove out of the driveway for the last time in our cherry red Volvo.

I am not a carrot. Joey and Mama are, though. They ended up in the soft ground. They're lucky. They're there while I'm still here stuck with the same orange hair I've come to associate with my favorite food. That strong, vibrant root vegetable, the carrot.

# Carrot-Spotting

*Jonathan Lethem*

Something I've very rarely been able to make anyone understand—I've rarely even tried!—is that when I was a child I was able to see what other children imagined themselves to be. I mean really see it. In fact, I had no choice. Walking to school, I'd glance at the sidewalks ahead of me and see a scattering, usually, of pirates and princesses, astronauts, mermaids and policemen, as well as any number of animals—lions and leopards and elephants, dragons and gryphons, sometimes a rhino or two. If I'd mention it to the child in question, they might confirm what I'd seen, or deny it, but it didn't matter. For me, the identification was lucid as daylight, and every day might as well have been Halloween.

Most special, I knew, and the rarest of sightings, were the vegetables. I only saw a few of those each school year. I always knew the vegetables had arrived at their identities for some special reason, out of some special need. These children weren't playing, they were solving something, reaching deep into their relationship to the natural order to draw up some bodily knowledge they needed to get through one day to the next. Tomatoes were seeking the sun. Greens were a nourishing tangle, a branched reaching out to mingle in emotional salad. Asparagus were the quiet strivers, unable to let anyone know how high they wished to reach. But the root vegetables, the potatoes, the carrots, they had my respect. Despite their solidity and familiarity, I knew they were after something unknowable. They wanted to live both above and below. I never met a carrot who wasn't deep.

Then there came the day when I ran into another child who wasn't transparent to me. A complete shock. There must have been something surprising about me, in turn, because the two of us stood on the sidewalk and contemplated one another for the longest time, both completely mystified, as if something completely taken for granted had been undone. At some point I remember thinking, "This must be the person who can see into me." And then, with a pop, like a soap bubble my special shimmering talent exploded and was gone. It was that day, when that other person looked into me, and I looked into them only enough to know they were looking into me, and I liked it, that I stopped being the child who saw the world as if every day was Halloween. It was that day that I gained an even more masterful superpower: I became a writer.

ALI MOHAMED, Hyenas
ELIZABETH GILBERT, Cheekbone

AMIRA AL SAMMRAI, Breathing in the Rain
RICHARD BLANCO, Burning in the Rain

CHRISTINA MURRAY, Carrots
JONATHAN LETHEM, Carrot-Spotting

**COLIN SHEPARD, Wildernesses**
**BILL ROORBACH, Heat Rises**

ELIAS NASRAT, The Fate of the Trees
BETSY SHOLL, That Leafless Tree

HASSAN JEYLANI, A Day in Three Worlds
CAMPBELL MCGRATH, Night and Day

JULIAN MAYORQUIN, Bottle Jacking
GEORGE SAUNDERS, Go to Jail, After Eight Times, Go Directly to Jail

RICHARD AKERA, I Started to Explain
RICHARD RUSSO, Drinking Water

VASSILY MURANGIRA, Swimming to Safety
ANN BEATTIE, Drive-by Alligator

JANET MATHIESON, A Sandwich/An Olive
ARI MEIL, Jammy Brightness

MAHAD HILOWLE, The Table
SUSAN CONLEY, The Table

DARCIE SERFES, The Bump
LILY KING, Summer

NOAH WILLIAMS, Hunting in the Deep Woods
LEWIS ROBINSON, When Dad Rode Past Me

MICHÉE RUNYAMBO, Two Teeth
MONICA WOOD, History Lesson

EMILY HOLLYDAY, Cantaloupe
GIBSON FAY-LEBLANC, Self-Portrait, with Dish Rag

MISSOURI ALICE WILLIAMS, A Little Secret
MELISSA COLEMAN, Goddess of Liberation

FADUMO ISSACK, Climbing Barefoot
JAED COFFIN, The Coconut Tree

GRACE WHITED, Box of Hope
DAVE EGGERS, Pull the Sled, Feed the Fire

AQILA SHARAFYAR, The Faithful Doves of My Father
SARA CORBETT, I Thought I Could Fix Things

ARUNA KENYI, The Photograph
MICHAEL PATERNITI, We Are Trying to Understand What Happened to You There

# Wildernesses

Colin Shepard

Anything can happen outside. Yesterday I saw an owl. I was walking home from school through a little patch of woods when I heard something fly up from behind a fence. I thought at first the owl was a crow, but then it occurred to me that crows aren't brown. The bird landed on the telephone wire and I got a good look at it. I was surprised to come across an owl in such a populated area, especially in daylight.

It reminded me of a time when we lived in Buxton, when I was five or six years old. One evening when I was letting my dog into the house I saw something big and white in a tree. I called my dad. He got a flashlight, and we saw that the shape in the tree was a huge snowy white owl, maybe two feet tall. My heart started beating faster. I wasn't scared, but I was excited. It had big black eyes, and the feathers around its eyes looked like white bowls. The beak was a kind of mustard yellow.

The next night I waited for it on the back porch, and watched through a sliding glass door. I didn't see the owl arrive, but at some point I looked up and it was there in the tree again. I told my dad and my grandmother that the owl was back. I watched it for a while, and then I left. That was the last time I saw the owl.

I like surprises. I like uncertainty and discovery. What makes me happy is the small things: the rivers I've found, the fish I've caught, the people I've met.

My grandmother died a while back. She used to let me help her cook, and she took me fishing. She loved to fish. She used to take me to a place where they had taken out a bridge. We'd fish from one side, and the current was so strong you couldn't always tell if you had a fish on your line or not. We caught buckets full of white perch. They were maybe six to eight inches long, with flat bodies and medium-size eyes. My grandmother would cook some of the fish and freeze the rest.

Now I usually fish by myself. While exploring on my own last year near Sebago Lake, I found an inlet behind a sandbar that created a sort of pond. I dragged my kayak across the sandbar and back into the inlet. I was in there fishing for two or three hours. I caught five or six bass; the biggest one was 2.5 pounds or so—a big fish for an area that small.

I was paddling along the shore, and a horse fly was following me around. It bit me a few times, and the bites swelled on my arms and legs. I tried killing it, swatting it away. It finally left.

My fishing pole was propped up next to me, and a huge black dragonfly with clear wings landed on the tip of the pole. I watched the dragonfly as my kayak coasted along the shoreline. Then the horsefly came back.

The dragonfly took off, and I heard its wings beating over to my right; then it landed on the front of the kayak. It had captured the horsefly and was eating it. The dragonfly's mouth was like two doors that opened from opposite sides of its head. The doors opened and shut as the dragonfly bit the horsefly. You could see the head of the dragonfly move. It ate the horsefly's abdomen first, and then the horsefly was gone.

I like surprises, but I don't want life to be too uncertain or too surprising. The horsefly's death was a good surprise—for me. Not for the horsefly.

There's another reason I like being outside. I like having the freedom to be as loud as I want; to go where I want to go. I like having time to reflect on my experience, time to think and maybe understand things I didn't understand before. No one else is around. I get a feeling, this really peaceful feeling, which kind of opens me up. I'm out in the middle of the woods where it's quiet. I can hear birds flying. If it just rained, water drips off the trees and I step into puddles.

What do I believe? I think that if you're not given freedom, you should take it. And if you have freedom, you should protect it. When I say freedom, I mean the freedom to do what you love.

# Heat Rises

*Bill Roorbach*

Everything happens outside. One winter night I was sitting at my desk in my studio—an old sugar shack—and something big landed on the roof—a branch? Clod of snow from the balsam firs overhead? Then came the hooting—"Who cooks for you? Who cooks for you? Who cooks for haaaaaarh!" I jumped a mile. Barred owl, with that madman's bark at the end of its call. He or she, I don't know, but it stayed the rest of the working evening, occasional calls (I jumped every time), flew off in great, physical silence when I stepped outside late.

It reminded me of a time skiing back in the woods here in Farmington, Maine, with Baila, our exuberant dog, heavy, heavy snow coming down. I was fifty or fifty-one years old. She ran ahead as always, and up there somewhere spooked an owl, who used the airspace above the path as a flyway through all the burdened trees—right at me, in other words, wingspan of near four feet, silence, though, otherworldly silence, that roundest of faces in brown feathers coming at me, a disk in shades, those deep eyes at it noticed me, its own mortality of no concern it seemed, though it seemed to see mine.

For the next decade—that is until now—I looked for that bird every time I went out. And I've seen it, or at least its fellows, quite a number of times, but never so dramatically.

I don't like surprises. I like certainty, more and more. Though that's a kind of surprise in itself, a discovery. What makes me happy is the big things—the rivers I've swum in, the fish I've seen, the people I've caught. Even those I had to throw back. With people, it's all catch-and-release.

My mother died a while ago. We kids—five of us in turn—baked with her when we were little, all sorts of cakes and pies and cookies, old school, one of those giant mixers with the huge, opaque mixing bowls, and beaters to lick. And Mom collected owls, all sorts of figurines and clocks and ashtrays, a great thing because it made it easy to buy a little gift for her. When she died I got there too late, but was able at least to sit with her body an hour by myself, pat her snowy hair. When I finally went outside (the funeral home guys were waiting), I walked up the hill in the backyard, back to the overlook over the bird sanctuary, a place I'd always played war with the neighbor kids. And a huge wingspan flew up, as snowy white as Mom. Snowy owl? What? But I looked into it when I was finally back home and found that there'd been an irruption, that large numbers of snowy owls were spending the winter south of their usual subarctic territory. Of course, I prefer to think the one I spotted was not an owl at all but a soul on its way to the next world.

I still like to bake. I love to make bread. I made sourdough for years and finally figured out how to make baguettes from it, real crunchy baguettes that crackled when you took them out of the oven, all but sang. But I don't eat a lot of bread these days, and haven't made any recently.

Oh, but once. Our kitchen can fill with houseflies. Empty for weeks, then suddenly the dozens. I was kneading bread and this one fly kept bombarding me—into my face, walk on my ear, up and down my arms, and me too covered with flour to swat at it. But when I was done kneading I washed my hands and washed the mixing bowl—this takes forever—got the dough back in it and into a warm corner to rise. Then I stood back at the counter, waited for my fly.

It landed on my forehead, walked down my nose, took a sharp left, walked down my cheek, hopped down onto the cutting board. I put my two hands out like playing a very small accordion, carefully placed them a foot apart, six inches above the cutting board, nicely centered over my tormentor. Then I clapped. I read somewhere that the fly instinct is to leap straight up, and it does seem to be true. The timing was perfect. A fly's last applause. Later, the bread was great, too.

I don't like surprises, but do like life to be surprising. My continuing satisfaction at killing that fly was a surprise. And that I felt no remorse.

Still, I'll take solitude over surprises.

What do I believe? Not much anymore. Heat rises. That's true. And that we all die. That's true, too. When I say believe, I guess I mean know. I've got five or six of my mom's owls on the windowsill in the kitchen, and every so often one takes me by surprise. That much I know for sure.

ALI MOHAMED, Hyenas
ELIZABETH GILBERT, Cheekbone

AMIRA AL SAMMRAI, Breathing in the Rain
RICHARD BLANCO, Burning in the Rain

CHRISTINA MURRAY, Carrots
JONATHAN LETHEM, Carrot-Spotting

COLIN SHEPARD, Wildernesses
BILL ROORBACH, Heat Rises

**ELIAS NASRAT, The Fate of the Trees**
**BETSY SHOLL, That Leafless Tree**

HASSAN JEYLANI, A Day in Three Worlds
CAMPBELL MCGRATH, Night and Day

JULIAN MAYORQUIN, Bottle Jacking
GEORGE SAUNDERS, Go to Jail, After Eight Times, Go Directly to Jail

RICHARD AKERA, I Started to Explain
RICHARD RUSSO, Drinking Water

VASSILY MURANGIRA, Swimming to Safety
ANN BEATTIE, Drive-by Alligator

JANET MATHIESON, A Sandwich/An Olive
ARI MEIL, Jammy Brightness

MAHAD HILOWLE, The Table
SUSAN CONLEY, The Table

DARCIE SERFES, The Bump
LILY KING, Summer

NOAH WILLIAMS, Hunting in the Deep Woods
LEWIS ROBINSON, When Dad Rode Past Me

MICHÉE RUNYAMBO, Two Teeth
MONICA WOOD, History Lesson

EMILY HOLLYDAY, Cantaloupe
GIBSON FAY-LEBLANC, Self-Portrait, with Dish Rag

MISSOURI ALICE WILLIAMS, A Little Secret
MELISSA COLEMAN, Goddess of Liberation

FADUMO ISSACK, Climbing Barefoot
JAED COFFIN, The Coconut Tree

GRACE WHITED, Box of Hope
DAVE EGGERS, Pull the Sled, Feed the Fire

AQILA SHARAFYAR, The Faithful Doves of My Father
SARA CORBETT, I Thought I Could Fix Things

ARUNA KENYI, The Photograph
MICHAEL PATERNITI, We Are Trying to Understand What Happened to You There

# The Fate of the Trees

*Elias Nasrat*

I.

An alley on the left
and a street in front
formed an angle
that embraced our home.

Across the street
grass
and
sessile trees
stared through the windows.

I know
why they stared, for
my father told me once
that our house
was a field.

The empty land
brought us, the neighborhood children,
together
we were home,
and safe,
as long as we were there.

We were the only ones
to worry about
the fate of the trees.
Otherwise, where would we hang
our swings? Or hide
from the sun on a hot summer's day
while we walked to school?

II.

I remember when we first moved
there was heavy snowfall.
Older children
took advantage of the land's shape
and built from it a slope.
I watched them from the window
or sometimes went along.

After winter, spring came:
The grass grew tall
and butterflies flew
from flower
to
flower.
The tall grass was
a better floor to fall on
than the dry hard floor of summer
or
the sloppy floor of winter.

When spring ended, summer came.
We hung our swings in the trees
or made ourselves soldiers
firing at each other
with water filled guns.
The older children did not care
what we did.
They flew kites instead.

Autumn made me feel alone,
not because my friends were gone—

there was something in the nature
of this season:
Maybe seeing
barren trees
and the sky clear . . .

III.

Now, years later
I live in another place.

Here,
there are three fields nearby our house:
One with full grass but no trees.
One with full grass surrounded by tall maples.
One with nothing
but tall trees.

When I was young I wished I would
grow up fast.
Now that I am older
the snow stays a long time
and I don't have time
to play outside.

# That Leafless Tree

*Betsy Sholl*

"Just like that," it said, "my leaves loosen
and leave. Inside, my pulpy rise slowly
subsides. Stems dry. In wind rush they flee
and scatter like scree. You ask what I am.

Woman, an *am,* not an *I.* You are an *I,* thinking
to make me speak. But is it me you seek,
or your own runes rutted into my trunk?
You who want so badly to be, it is not a *me*

before you, but a stretch, a reach, from root
to leaf, thick to thin, and less—an *is* and *what if,*
as much hidden as seen, an *under* as much
as *above,* a groping down, till root tips

melt into earth, a slow ooze into other.
Is that what you wanted to hear, you who
have no roots, only shadows, who want
with words alone and no loss to be lifted up?"

It asked in a scratchy voice, or I heard.
Then wordless went out to feel how other
it was, how real, that guardian, elder,
sentry at my window, that leafless tree.

ALI MOHAMED, Hyenas
ELIZABETH GILBERT, Cheekbone

AMIRA AL SAMMRAI, Breathing in the Rain
RICHARD BLANCO, Burning in the Rain

CHRISTINA MURRAY, Carrots
JONATHAN LETHEM, Carrot-Spotting

COLIN SHEPARD, Wildernesses
BILL ROORBACH, Heat Rises

ELIAS NASRAT, The Fate of the Trees
BETSY SHOLL, That Leafless Tree

**HASSAN JEYLANI, A Day in Three Worlds**
**CAMPBELL MCGRATH, Night and Day**

JULIAN MAYORQUIN, Bottle Jacking
GEORGE SAUNDERS, Go to Jail, After Eight Times, Go Directly to Jail

RICHARD AKERA, I Started to Explain
RICHARD RUSSO, Drinking Water

VASSILY MURANGIRA, Swimming to Safety
ANN BEATTIE, Drive-by Alligator

JANET MATHIESON, A Sandwich/An Olive
ARI MEIL, Jammy Brightness

MAHAD HILOWLE, The Table
SUSAN CONLEY, The Table

DARCIE SERFES, The Bump
LILY KING, Summer

NOAH WILLIAMS, Hunting in the Deep Woods
LEWIS ROBINSON, When Dad Rode Past Me

MICHÉE RUNYAMBO, Two Teeth
MONICA WOOD, History Lesson

EMILY HOLLYDAY, Cantaloupe
GIBSON FAY-LEBLANC, Self-Portrait, with Dish Rag

MISSOURI ALICE WILLIAMS, A Little Secret
MELISSA COLEMAN, Goddess of Liberation

FADUMO ISSACK, Climbing Barefoot
JAED COFFIN, The Coconut Tree

GRACE WHITED, Box of Hope
DAVE EGGERS, Pull the Sled, Feed the Fire

AQILA SHARAFYAR, The Faithful Doves of My Father
SARA CORBETT, I Thought I Could Fix Things

ARUNA KENYI, The Photograph
MICHAEL PATERNITI, We Are Trying to Understand What Happened to You There

# A Day in Three Worlds

*Hassan Jeylani*

I wake to the sound of my dad's alarm clock—it's loud, insistent, like a fire alarm. I'm in bed, wrapped up in two or three blankets, and through the doorway I see my dad shaking his head while he tries to loop his tie. I sit up. My clock reads 7:11 A.M. I rub my eyes—am I dreaming, or is my dad actually there, getting ready? He walks over toward me, still adjusting his tie.

"Get up, it's Sunday," he says.

"Huh?"

"It's Sunday, Hassan, get up."

I'm still asleep, but the thought of my dad dressing up on a Sunday morning and telling me to get up puzzles me. I pull my blankets back over my head and pretend this isn't happening.

He comes back again. He goes to my brother's bed this time, knowing it'll take more than words to get him up. My dad hits my brother's shoulders several times, and Kahiye jumps to his feet.

"I'm awake, I'm awake . . . The bus doesn't leave for twenty minutes. I've got time," my brother says, still asleep.

My dad laughs, "*Waryaatha*, it's Eid, get ready, prayers are about to start."

\* \* \*

I had forgotten Eid, the most joyful Muslim holiday. For fifteen years I've been celebrating Eid, anticipating it each year. But this year, I didn't wake up with that same excitement. I didn't even know it was Eid until my dad told me. How could I have forgotten?

For most Muslims, Eid is one of the most important days of the year. It comes a couple weeks after Ramadan, which is thirty days of fasting and is one of the five pillars a Muslim must follow in his lifetime. At fifteen, Muslim boys and girls are expected to fast for Ramadan—the fasting allows Muslims to get out of their ordinary lives and put themselves in someone else's shoes. At fifteen, we are supposed to have sworn that there's only one God. At fifteen, we're supposed to do the five daily prayers. At fifteen, if possible, we're supposed to give back to the poor. At fifteen, we're supposed to be dreaming about going on the Hajj once in our lives.

At fifteen, I barely complete the days of Ramadan. At fifteen, I struggle to do the five daily prayers. At fifteen, I don't have a job or any money to give back to anyone.

\* \* \*

"Allaahu Akbar, Allaahu Akbar, Allaahu Akbar."

I am in the third row, sitting with my legs crossed, my arms on my thighs, repeating the ritual words of the imam. I am wearing *cimmamad* and *qamiis* and a hat, the traditional Muslim clothes. We're in the gym at Portland High School, and we have all brought our own prayer mats. There are sixty or seventy of us praying with the imam, fewer people than last year. The men pray at the front, and where normally there would be a curtain or a wall, instead there's just a space, and the women pray behind it. As prayers are about to start, a few little boys are running around near where their mothers will stand and pray. I laugh—when I was their age, I was well dressed and stood next to my dad and prayed with everyone else. When I was their age, I prayed five times a day.

Prayers are optional right now. Not because I've lost faith, but because of the society I live in. Also, I forget it takes fewer than two minutes. My mind is set up to go to school, come home, and go to sleep.

\* \* \*

In Somalia, where I was born and lived for the first two years of my life, on Eid we woke up in the morning and went to morning prayers. The stores, the businesses, the meat market, even the guy who walked around with a large covered plate selling sweet candy, took a day off—everything was shut down for the entire day. Morning prayers were at the mosque, and everyone was there dressed in their traditional clothes.

The inside of the mosque was beautiful, the ceiling was decorated with gold and other bright colors, and the windows were open. I think about a thousand people fit in there. It was huge. All these people crammed together sat on a massive rug covering the floor with the Koran in their laps.

There is an imam at the front. The prayer takes a few minutes, depending on the imam. Nowadays, little kids are with their moms, but I remember being with my dad. The women aren't in the back in Somalia, they're completely separate, in a separate room.

After the prayer, you look to the left and to the right and say something that's almost like "Merry Christmas." Then the kids walk around and get money from everyone. After that, I go back to my home, and then I am free to do whatever I want. There's no school that day or the next day. I try to get out of my traditional clothes.

I go outside, walk around. Everyone's out, doing their own thing, sitting under apple and banana trees for the shade. Some kids are playing soccer in the sand. My dad has changed out of his work clothes, and he's wearing the Somali version of a sarong, sitting on a low stool with jugs of water all around him. It's sort of like you're in the mall, but everyone knows each other and would say—no matter if you were rich, poor, crippled—that Allah was there, God was there, and you're worshipping Him.

* * *

During the war in Somalia, when I was two, my family had flown to Kenya to get away from the chaos. My parents hope to return, but they knew there is a slim chance of going back.

In Nairobi, there weren't very many Muslims around. As a kid, I'd think, "I'm gonna go pray, if I want, go to school, then maybe go play a little soccer." Eid still happened there, but you didn't get that same sense you had in Somalia. Nairobi was so huge, and we lived in the city. The people there were all different. I wasn't used to huge buildings, and it was very busy.

I remember one time in Nairobi when a girl my older brother's age, Marion, burst through the gate where my brother and I were playing soccer, saying, "Let's play." We'd just finished playing one-touch pass, so they got some other older kids to play with them. At three, I knew I was too little to play a pick-up game. Just before the game got started, Marion said, "I need someone to watch out for my dad." Being a Muslim girl, Marion wasn't allowed to play with guys.

Kahiye told me to be the lookout. I climbed up on the tall iron fence and stood sideways on a little ledge watching both the game and for Marion's father. I could see over the fence, my head just above the fence's sharp points. I watched as Marion put the ball between Kahiye's legs and then ran around him and scored. As I watched Marion dancing around the goal, I saw out of the corner of my eye Marion's father walking to the gate. In the excitement of the goal and the fear that Marion would never be able to play again, with my hands gripping the fence points, I tried to jump down, and one of the points sliced my neck.

I fell flat on my back. I saw birds overhead in the clear, hot sky, my head spinning. My brother picked me up and held me up to his chest and, when he let me back down, blood, my blood, covered his shirt.

* * *

This memory runs through my mind as I walk over to the Y here in Portland to play basketball with my friends, brother, and cousins. This has been my home now for eight years. I change into my basketball shorts and my Jermaine O'Neal high-tops and one of my practice jerseys. My cousins are shooting for teams as I come back from the bathroom. As soon as I see them, I drop to the ground laughing.

"Yo, quit playing around. Get changed," I say.

"We're ready, man, c'mon," Mustaf says.

Mustaf's got jeans, a black tanktop, and dress-up shoes on. Omar's wearing a white button-down shirt, khaki shorts, and sandals.

"Alright, forget it, let's just play," I say.

What I don't say is that I remember when I was like that, not knowing what to wear, not being used to having so many different kinds of clothes to choose from.

We're playing four on four, full court. Shots are falling for everyone. We're sort of like the "And1" team: it's all about street ball, crossing someone up, throwing no-look passes, talking mad trash. I'm at center court, holding the ball, and then Omar's covering me. I look down and laugh at his sandals. I shake him to the right, and he doesn't react. I shake him to the left, and he still doesn't react. I take off to the right full speed, and I can hear his sandals chasing after me. I cross the ball back over to my left hand and for a second I don't hear the flapping of his sandals. Then I hear him drop flat on his ass.

The game stops. I stop. I drop the ball and start laughing. Everyone hovers over him, booing and laughing at how badly he's been faked.

* * *

Kahiye and I are back at home, collapsed on the couches, playing FIFA 2006 on PlayStation 2, still laughing about Omar and his sandals. After a few games, Kahiye gets tired of losing and turns off the system and goes to fix something to eat. I flip through the channels and put on ESPN. During SportsCenter, there's a commercial for the latest DVD collection of *Baywatch*. Pamela Anderson running down the beach in her signature red swimsuit.

It was in Nairobi when I started watching American movies and *Baywatch*. In Somalia, we didn't have a TV in the house where we lived. We couldn't believe it. Money, cars, houses, all this stuff, Pamela Anderson running by in a bikini—TV gave us our ideas about America. We thought in the U.S. everything was handed to you, like gold. You'd get your own house, your own car, a pool.

I remember sitting on my bunk bed in Nairobi, cramped in a small room with my family. It was so hot that we kept checking the fan to see if it was on. It was always on. A commercial would lure us in, showing a fancy house with a pool. Our fantasies would take over. We were living in a mansion in America, my sisters were in the pool while my brother and I were in the house being served by Jeffrey, the butler from the *Fresh Prince of Bel Air*. "Dinner is served, Master Hassan," he would say.

The commercial ends. Kahiye is banging the fan.

* * *

Later, I decide to pray Isha, the last prayer of the day. It takes a couple minutes to do the ritual movements, most of which involve standing, bowing, kneeling, and placing my head on the floor. I used to do it almost every day, but most nights now I run out of time.

After I'm done, I sit on my bed, hands held up high, reciting parts of the Koran. I lie on my back looking at the ceiling and let my mind wander. This is when all the doubts and questions I have start to unfold.

I prayed five times a day in Somalia. In Nairobi, three times. Now, it's none. It's not consistent. The religion is still here, people are here. Prayers and traditions are still here. But Eid's not a holiday, or at least it doesn't feel like it.

Most of the changes have happened because of where we are. If I were in Somalia, things would be less complicated: get up, pray, eat, go to Muslim school, come home, eat, go back to prayer. There, every day revolves around the same quotidian existence. In Somalia, prayer was most important.

I do stop once in a while and think about it. I don't want to forget a single homework assignment. I don't want to forget a single prayer. I don't want to forget a single basketball practice. There are consequences to all three. But there's not enough time to do all three. I even ask for help from religious leaders.

"I can't handle school, I can't handle basketball, I can't handle my religion all at once," I say. "How I should balance all of them?" The same answer always comes back: the Koran. In other words, they want me to seek answers myself.

My dad wanted to get us away from the tribal fighting in Somalia. I've started my whole life over. I've gone from having to share a room to having my own. I've gone from having no TV to two TVs and a computer and an iPod. I've gone from barefoot to nine different kinds of shoes. I've gone from three outfits to a closet full of them.

I appreciate all these precious things and the opportunities I've been given, but there's an empty hole in my life. I've gained all these things, but I've lost something and I want to recover it. Most nights I fall asleep thinking about all this, but then, two days later, I'm playing basketball at the Y and thinking about Omar and Mustaf, and these thoughts are gone.

# NIGHT AND DAY

*CAMPBELL MCGRATH*

Last year, during the month of Ramadan, my family and I spent ten days traveling in Turkey. The crowds that gathered in central Istanbul to celebrate the evening meal astonished us—huge, celebratory family groups, with samovars and hampers and picnic blankets, platters of food sealed in plastic wrap, awaiting sunset and the muezzin's call to break the fast. It felt like the Fourth of July on the mall in Washington D.C., where I grew up, repeated night after night, with the spectacle of fireworks replaced by the simpler act of breaking bread, one a secular occasion, the other spiritual, together sharing the bonds of community and faith. Later we stayed in the hill town of Sirince, where we were awakened before dawn by the man who strolled the steep cobbled alleyways banging a big drum, as if trying out for a high school marching band. Lacking the mosques and minarets of Istanbul, this was a more effective way of reaching the scattered farms and cottages with news of the impending sunrise, when the daylong fast would begin anew.

What a beautiful place that was, a valley of cross-hatched farms and orchards with old blue tractors towing crates of cucumbers and gigantic peaches to market, beat-up orange motor cycles with battered flatbed sidecars carrying huge tin cans of olive oil; long thin peppers strung on front porches below new TV dishes, drying in the sun, green to orange to red; goats and donkeys, wasps and blackberries, the big farm dog that followed us home and jumped through the window into our courtyard; walking down the hill in the heat of the afternoon for bread and olives and fig jelly and tea; searching for August meteors in a quilt of stars before the moon rose over the ridge like a cosmic hunk of honeydew melon.

Fasting and feasting, developed and undeveloped, spiritual and secular, past and present—so many dualities, these binary pairings we utilize to organize and explain the world and our lived experiences. This is the poem summoned up by one such pair and the thoughts and memories they set in motion.

## Night and Day

Day is as simple as the body,
night is like the mind.
Day is water, night is wine.

Day is a flock of sparrows,
night is an owl.
Day is a consonant, night is a vowel.

Night is the sacred cat of the Egyptians,
day is a dog, any old dog.
Night is the salt in the day's wide ocean.
Day is bread, night is fog.

# Bottle Jacking

*Julian Mayorquin*

*There's a hill in my neighborhood, and a basketball court at the bottom. When you're sitting on the hill you overlook the court, and when you head up it you're heading out of Riverton. I guess Gale was coming into Riverton, over the hill, with another friend of mine who works with him over at Big Lots. He got out of the car, took the BB gun out, and while wearing his ankle bracelet, he shot our friend Julius ten times in the face.*

My neighborhood is Portland Housing in Riverton—it is a close-knit little community of minorities. I was friends with these two kids named Ghee and Gale who also lived there. The story I want to tell is about Gale. He was my best friend. He was the person I'd wake up, call, and see what's going on. I'd stay at his house at night. His mom knew me.

I got to know Gale in middle school. He moved to Riverton in seventh grade, and we played this game called Booty. In Booty, you'd hold on to the pole of the basketball hoop and bend over, and if you got tipped, you'd fall over on your butt. I got 150 booties on Gale, and it escalated like that until he just gave up and one day was like, "Yo, come to my house and I'll give you food. Please, just no more booties." And so I went to his house and we ate ice cream. Soon we'd become good friends and we'd hang out all the time and just kick it. He'd sleep over my house, and I'd sleep over his, but after he got into drinking and weed that became his priority.

In eighth grade, I was just getting into smoking weed myself when I got Gale into it. We used to get together before the bus came every day, and we'd smoke. We'd smoke to go to school, and we'd smoke after school and go on wild adventures. We'd done this for months, and when the school year was finally over, we started experimenting with drinking, and when we started drinking, some kids kind of took it to their heads; Gale, too.

He started going bottle jacking. Some people have strategy, but not the kids I knew who did it; it was just thug life and the idea was that you could just have it all. They went to Hannaford by the Bay and Shaw's Northgate, Hannaford Falmouth . . . it didn't matter, just any neighborhood store that sold liquor. They stole six or seven bottles, extreme amounts of bottles, at a time. They'd tend to wear big clothes, because it was kind of the style anyway, and they'd just walk into the aisle and grab bottles, stuff them into their clothes, and walk out. And it didn't matter how it went off, it didn't matter if you were getting chased, you just got the bottles.

Bottle jacking started affecting everything. We had so much alcohol that we were drunk all the time, and being drunk meant we thought we could do anything. We started breaking into people's cars, stealing things. As the summer wore on, it became more and more of an everyday thing. Then, we were back in school, and we'd get bottles and skip the whole day of school, just drunk.

By the time we had transitioned to high school Gale was a different person. He became really greedy and it was already taking a toll on his life. He was on probation—I'm on probation still, everyone was on probation—but the drinking didn't stop. Gale got caught smoking and drinking in school and got involved with the cops and he'd stop going home so they couldn't find him. Instead he'd go to somebody's house where he could just smoke and drink all night.

I couldn't be like that because I have a really, really hardcore mom. She's like really old school, old school Hispanic. She sticks to these rules: You live in this house, you sleep in this house, this is where you are. So while my crew would be partying at night, I'd be home. Gale, he was killing his relationship with his mom. He lost all respect for her because she told his P.O. all of his problems. First, it was house arrest. Then it was a couple of times that he had violated probation, and then, out of nowhere, Gale was in Long Creek Correctional.

*We're all seventeen now. All five of the kids that were a part of the crew with me back in the day ended up in jail. It was just Raul, a younger kid, a sibling who just followed us around, and me who stayed out. Ghee sobered up. Julius doesn't live with his family; he lives a long way from home, like in Lewiston. He's in some program. Amman's in a group home. David's in rehab. And Gale's in jail, committed till he's twenty-one.*

There is this lady in my neighborhood that people call Freak. She's thirty-five to forty-five, a grown woman, she has four kids, and she gets around the neighborhood. We call her Freak because she's a freak, she's a whore, and she's a pedophile. And people laugh about it, but the reality is not too funny. She and Gale had a relationship at some point, and he would always deny it, but on those nights that he would sneak out, he would go to Freak's house.

At about that time, his P.O. got word that there was a warrant out for his arrest. They were coming to get him. For two months Gale was on the run, but the whole time he stayed in Riverton at this lady's house. After a long while, he decided he could go home, but when he got there, his mom turned him in. That's when he went to jail again.

By the time he got out of jail the second time, he wasn't the same Gale at all anymore. He wasn't the guy I used to hang with, play Avatar with, or other little kid games. Jail changed him. He was gritty. It was sad, because he'd been such a good friend of mine. He continued to have a thing with this lady. He used her for money and stayed at her house. He didn't care about trying to go home again. His P.O. caught him smoking, and he went to jail again, and when he got out this time he said he wouldn't smoke or drink, that he would check in, but he just went back to drinking and smoking, and really, that became his life. His P.O. put him in ankle weights on house arrest, and he got a job at Big Lots, but he still spent all his time at Freak's house, and would get away with it by telling his P.O. that he had a job babysitting her kids.

At this point, I didn't have much of a relationship with Gale. We'd smoke a little together, and we'd reminisce about the past, but he wasn't the same person and we didn't have much to say to one another. Julius, one of the friends who was with us during the whole bottle jacking thing, used to come down from Lewiston sometimes to visit with his mom and dad. Well, I guess he hung out with Freak one of those times. Gale heard about it and he flipped out on Julius. The whole neighborhood was shocked because Julius was one of his boys. Gale was still mad about it, and he ended up shooting Julius in the face, close range, from only a couple feet away, with a BB gun.

*I don't know what Gale was thinking. He just went about his day, but the cops got all of the information, and they came, ended up bagging him back at work, at Big Lots, four cops cuffing him right there. And now what I hear is that he's going to be in jail for the next four years. Till he's twenty-one. From seventeen until twenty-one. This kid was my best friend. And this all started by smoking a couple of bowls before catching the bus to Lincoln Middle School. And I introduced him to it.*

Our friend Ghee went that way, too, spending a lot of time in jail. But when I look at Ghee now, I see this whole other side. Like as hard as it was for Ghee, he's sobered up, he's clean now. He doesn't smoke, he doesn't drink. He's satisfied with where he is. But Gale is doing it the hard way, and he's locked up.

And what about me? I still smoke. I don't drink as much. I'm not hardcore. My day does not revolve around smoking or drinking. I know I should quit drinking. At one point I was drinking pretty heavily. It didn't matter what day it was, I just wanted to get drunk. I didn't want to think about things. I got fired from Arby's because of drinking. And it was sad, too, because it was a week after that I found out that my friend died of a heroin overdose.

This all happened a couple of months ago. And ever since then it's just been a negative downslope. My girlfriend just told me she was moving to Florida. She's leaving in seventeen days. A junkie pawned my iPhone. I got taken in a scam on Craigslist for my Xbox. My relationship with my dad has completely deteriorated. I don't talk to him anymore. I spent a couple months with him this summer. I was the only one of his kids that helped him move down to Jacksonville, Florida, and the whole trip was filled with hollow promises. I was discouraged by that and didn't feel like talking to him, but then when my phone got robbed I couldn't talk to him anyway.

*Do you know about The Secret? It's all about replacing negative thoughts with happy ones. It's from this book, from a documentary; this guy I know had it. It teaches you to be grateful for what you have, and to picture what you want and really believe in it, and to see yourself with it. I really want to study political science, and I want to go to an Ivy League school, so I'm just going to try to keep this mentality to get there. I'm just trying to stay happy about things. I have all of these negative things happening, so I feel like The Secret is my last thing. It's my only hope. So I got to stick with it.*

Whenever I start to get down I just think about my nephew. My brother's girlfriend had a kid on Labor Day. And he's the first of us three to have a baby. So, he's keeping me up. Just knowing he's there, and knowing he's doing good—that's everything. I can see him whenever I want, but I don't get to see him too much because he lives in South Portland, which is kind of far, and my mom, she works like two, three jobs. She's a hardworking lady, and she's always working and then always sleeping. We have a different relationship. We have a lot to work on.

I'm just going to try to concentrate on getting a job, and working out, staying healthy. Keeping The Secret. I'm just going to keep believing in that. I'm going to succeed. It's going to happen. I'm just going to keep believing and keep my head up. I guess I could see all of this as a fresh start. I'm just in a big hole, but there's no way to go except up. I've got a smile on my face.

# Go to Jail, After Eight Times, Go Directly to Jail

*George Saunders*

In the temporary detention center at the Laredo North Border Patrol Station, a Mexican kid slumps in a chair at a processing desk. He's going to jail for at least three months, because this is the eighth time he'd been caught illegally entering the United States and the system's patience has finally been exhausted.

Border Patrol Agent One runs a hand shyly over his new haircut, which is nearly a buzz.

"That, see, I don't understand that haircut," says Agent Two, wearing a cowboy hat.

"At least he's *got* hair," says Agent Three, and Agent Two blushes, acknowledging it: Yes, yes, it's true. Under this hat, I'm bald.

I point to my own head.

We all laugh at my hairline.

Then I look over at the kid. He's sitting there expressionless, a small cat among large dogs. And now he's got to endure this balding talk, this nervous braying laughter, before he can get to the next enjoyable step (being processed), and on to the part where he gets sent off to a foreign jail.

My heart goes out to him.

Sort of.

Because empathy depends on how you've spent your day. I've just spent mine driving around in a "marked caged unit" with Agent Three, aka Dan Garibay: visiting the muddy clearings where illegal aliens change into dry clothes after they cross, inspecting fence-cuts, driving past safe houses, hearing agents talk about tracking groups of illegals for eleven straight hours. I've learned that it's now more profitable to traffic in humans than in drugs; that MS-13, a Salvadoran gang, is in a death struggle with the more traditional Mexican Mafia; that Border Patrol agents in Laredo are routinely shadowed by spies from the smuggling cartels who, in turn, are shadowed by a newly formed countersurveillance unit.

My relation to this Mexican kid, then, is something like that of a plumber's apprentice to a leak.

Dan's third-generation Mexican American, a funny, reasonable guy who seems to be constantly considering and reconsidering the moral implications of his job. He's got nothing against illegal aliens, understands why they do what they do, has compassionate feelings toward them, and seems committed to catching them in a way that keeps them safe and leaves their dignity intact. But the law is the law, and why should those who break the law be privileged over those who've played by the rules?

So I find myself thinking, re this silent (sullen? unrepentant?) kid, this member of *Wascals Who Insist on Trying to Elude My New Friend Dan*: Dude, what did you expect? *Seven times?* Who doesn't learn after seven times? Do you value your freedom so lightly? Do you have a wife, kids? Do you realize you are now going to miss the next three months of their—

Then, imagining that he has kids, who look like little Mexican versions of my kids back when they were toddlers, I (finally) experience a little heart-pang as I flash on what I'd be thinking if I were him: Laugh it up, you balding bastards, I'm dying here, can't you tell I'm a decent person, oh Jesus, please let me go, just this one last time, they're so cute and will never be this age again, please please, I've made a terrible mistake.

And what will you do if we let you go? I ask him in my mind. Will you try to get in here again? Next time, you could be looking at *five years*.

He hesitates, averts his eyes.

Seriously? I say. My God, is it worth it? Are things really that bad where you live?

And he just looks at me, as if to say: Would I keep trying if it didn't make sense to keep trying, if the possible reward didn't justify possibly getting caught? Do I look stupid?

He doesn't look stupid. He looks handsome and sad and ashamed.

But mostly what he looks like is: busted.

Busted, and waiting to pay the price.

ALI MOHAMED, Hyenas
ELIZABETH GILBERT, Cheekbone

AMIRA AL SAMMRAI, Breathing in the Rain
RICHARD BLANCO, Burning in the Rain

CHRISTINA MURRAY, Carrots
JONATHAN LETHEM, Carrot-Spotting

COLIN SHEPARD, Wildernesses
BILL ROORBACH, Heat Rises

ELIAS NASRAT, The Fate of the Trees
BETSY SHOLL, That Leafless Tree

HASSAN JEYLANI, A Day in Three Worlds
CAMPBELL MCGRATH, Night and Day

JULIAN MAYORQUIN, Bottle Jacking
GEORGE SAUNDERS, Go to Jail, After Eight Times, Go Directly to Jail

**RICHARD AKERA, I Started to Explain**
**RICHARD RUSSO, Drinking Water**

VASSILY MURANGIRA, Swimming to Safety
ANN BEATTIE, Drive-by Alligator

JANET MATHIESON, A Sandwich/An Olive
ARI MEIL, Jammy Brightness

MAHAD HILOWLE, The Table
SUSAN CONLEY, The Table

DARCIE SERFES, The Bump
LILY KING, Summer

NOAH WILLIAMS, Hunting in the Deep Woods
LEWIS ROBINSON, When Dad Rode Past Me

MICHÉE RUNYAMBO, Two Teeth
MONICA WOOD, History Lesson

EMILY HOLLYDAY, Cantaloupe
GIBSON FAY-LEBLANC, Self-Portrait, with Dish Rag

MISSOURI ALICE WILLIAMS, A Little Secret
MELISSA COLEMAN, Goddess of Liberation

FADUMO ISSACK, Climbing Barefoot
JAED COFFIN, The Coconut Tree

GRACE WHITED, Box of Hope
DAVE EGGERS, Pull the Sled, Feed the Fire

AQILA SHARAFYAR, The Faithful Doves of My Father
SARA CORBETT, I Thought I Could Fix Things

ARUNA KENYI, The Photograph
MICHAEL PATERNITI, We Are Trying to Understand What Happened to You There

# I Started to Explain

*Richard Akera*

I killed a dog once. When I was about thirteen, my brother Francis and I were coming back from getting water from the water fountain, and I was carrying a twenty-liter jerry can when I heard people yelling from a distance. I asked Francis, "What do you think is going on in the neighborhood"?

"I don't know," he said.

I heard my five-year-old brother Elvis before I saw him. "Mom, Mom!" he screamed, in the way he had of calling our mother's name whenever he was hurt or frightened or in trouble. Then I saw him.

Elvis was lying on the ground. The dog had bitten some of his teeth off, his lip was cracked open, his tongue had a hole in it, and he was bleeding everywhere.

The dog stood next to my brother as if he were ready to bite into him again. He was an old red dog, huge, twice Elvis's size. I was so scared when I first saw Elvis' face and so mad at the dog. I knew I had to kill this dog before it bit another person, and I left Elvis with Francis and some neighbors. My mother was not around; she had left for church that afternoon.

Rocks lay on the ground. I got some and started running after the dog. I was so mad; I wanted to catch it and take all of its teeth and eyes out, so that it wouldn't be able to see anymore or bite anyone again. I wanted to squeeze the life out of it. I was running after the dog and throwing rocks like a crazy man. And I was crying like a baby. I had no shoes, no sandals, no nothing. I never even noticed stepping on sharp objects. I did not notice anything, not until I killed the dog.

My neighbor Kizito was there with me, helping me catch the dog. Kizito, a strong guy who lived across the street from me, was holding this huge stake;

he kept throwing it at the dog and picking it up again. The dog ran into the banana plants next to my landlord's house. Kizito threw his stake again. "I think I broke its leg," he said. And he did, because after he hit the dog, it was not running that fast anymore and it got weaker and weaker.

I ran fast enough to hit it on the head with a stone. It fell down but I didn't stop hitting it. I was kicking it, and continued hitting it on the head to make sure it was dead and gone. And I was crying, and crying, and crying. "You bit my brother, you go to hell! You mess with my brother, you get to pay for it." Kizito was trying to stop me, and people were stopping their cars and staring at me like I was a crazy person.

"I think it's dead now," Kizito said.

"No!" I cried louder. "It's not yet dead!" I wanted to cut its head off to make sure it was really dead. Like dead-dead.

*  *  *

Meanwhile my landlady called her husband, my landlord Ssero, and told him what happened. Ssero came to take me to get my mom from the church. Before you knew it, we were there. At first I couldn't believe my own eyes. There were thousands of people in the church, and some people were even sitting outside because the church was so full. Others were standing by the road and watching what was going on in the church as it was projected on a big blackout cloth screen. It was crazy to me to see people right then who were so happy. A lot of them were just crying with the joy of worshipping and praying to God, who at this moment I didn't believe existed. If God were really there, if God were real, why would he let something so bad happen to a five-year-old kid?

When I finally found my mother she too was smiling, dancing, singing, and just praising the Lord. Her face looked like she was from heaven, like she was with the angels. Yet before you knew it, all the joy and happiness and maybe her beliefs would be gone.

"What are you guys doing here?" she said, still singing and clapping.

"Mom?" I called her.

"Yes," she replied with joyful voice.

"Mom, Elvis got bit by a dog."

For a moment, there was this silence, her face turned red, and she stopped clapping and singing and dancing. "Wha . . . what . . . what are you trying to tell me?"

"Elvis, he got bit by a dog," I repeated.

"But, how? How could this happen?" Her voice was shaking, and her body too.

"Are you okay, Mama Elvis?" the landlord asked.

"Am I okay? How can I be okay, when I just found out that a dog bit my baby? Please, God, don't take my boy away from me, not now!" she yelled.

I was afraid for her. I could see that she was broken. I could see that she was bleeding from the inside. "A mother's heart is never . . ." The taxi ride back to Elvis was a blur. When we got home, Elvis had been moved from where the dog bit him. My landlady and my brothers Francis and Fidele and the neighbors were around him. He was bleeding. There was a lot of talking around him. "Oh my God, is he going to be okay?" I heard someone say. My mother got out of the taxi and she started running toward the avocado tree where my brother was lying. She worked her way closer to Elvis. As soon as she saw him, she started crying. "How did this happen to my boy?"

She looked straight at me. I started to explain. I told her that only a few hours after she left, Elvis was crying, needing something to eat. I told her that I went to the neighbors to ask if I could get them some water, so I could buy something for Elvis. Before I could finish, she slapped me across the cheek.

\* \* \*

I wasn't really crying because of the slap, I was crying for my brother, watching him bleed and suffer like that. I was crying for myself, not from the pain of the slap, but because it was all my fault that the dog bit my brother. I was crying because I was trying to do something that would make my mom proud of me, because I had been trying to get something for my brothers to eat, by asking my neighbors if I could get water for them so I could bring back some bread or rice and cook it for us.

I was crying for all the ways my brothers and I tried to get even a little bit of money to get some food, searching the streets and along the railroad tracks for anything we could sell—bicycle parts, soda cans, water bottles; digging up the ground for pieces of scrap metal; climbing trees to find ripe jackfruit and avocados to sell door to door; helping out at the Sudanese Church, whose monthly parties we could hardly wait for. There we could make money carrying jerry cans of water, cleaning out the church, and helping to cook.

I was crying for the time when my mother had to go out and look for a job to wash people's clothes. I was crying because of the time when she had to go door to door, selling *getengy* or batiks or sarongs. I was crying because she is always out in the hot sun all day and has to walk most of the time because she doesn't have money for the taxi. She would come home with back pain, and you want to know what was funny? She would smile all the time telling us that it was going to be okay, but in my heart I knew that things were far from being okay; I knew it was never going to be okay, at least not too soon.

The thing was, she was trying to hide it from my brothers and me. She was wounded and she was dying. I could see it on her face; I knew she could use some help, but who could help her? I could tell that she was hurting, and it always bothered me to see her go through all of the pain alone. I felt horrible about myself, that I couldn't do anything to help her out, but just sit back and witness her bleed from the inside. My mother, a woman whose pulchritude was once admired by many, was now being talked about behind her back. Before, she would turn the heads of every man passing by the street of Kikony. A woman who had black natural hair and smooth brown skin, my mother now seemed to be fading away. All because of the stress she was under. After my dad died in 2005, my mother had to take over; she was now like both the man and the woman of the house at the same time. She was doing it all. And I was crying for her.

I was crying because of the embarrassment that my brothers and I had to go through, going to a boarding school that was across the street of Makerere Kikony to ask for leftovers, so that we could have something to put in our mouths. I had to watch my younger brothers cry because they had gone two or three days without eating anything, just drinking water; and what did I do? Nothing. I just sat there and sometimes joined in and started to cry with them, too.

I was crying for the hunger, for my mother, for the embarrassment; I was crying for the three months my brother would have to spend in a hospital, having operations on his face and his tongue. I was crying because of all the shit in my life. All of this, I mean the hunger, the suffering, the dog bite, made me ask, "Does God really exist? And if He does, where is He when we need Him the most? Why isn't He doing anything?"

# Drinking Water

*Richard Russo*

FADE IN ON:

EXT. LARGE PUBLIC FOUNTAIN - DAY

Water BURBLING. Into the frame comes a blue wooden bucket. A brown hand submerges it into the fountain and we CUT TO:

EXT. FOUNTAIN - SAME

From above, now, we see two skinny black boys at the fountain. The first looks to be about thirteen. The other is a couple years younger. It takes both of them to pull the full bucket out of the fountain by its handle. When they set it down in the dirt, water sloshes over the brim. They wait for the water to stop sloshing.

The bottom of the screen reads: REFUGEE CAMP. KAMPALA, UGANDA.

> OLDER BOY'S VOICEOVER
> I killed a dog once.

EXT. REFUGEE CAMP - SAME

The two boys struggle among the crowded tents with the heavy bucket of water. This is hard work, and both are sweating profusely in the hot sun.

Nearby, a COMMOTION, which attracts the attention of the older boy.

> VOICE IN THE DISTANCE
> (terrified)
> Mom! Mom!

The two boys set down the bucket and run toward the commotion.

> OLDER BOY
> (screams)
> Elvis!

EXT. CAMP - SAME

A sobbing boy, no more than five years old, lies in the dirt covered with blood. A large dog, red with a graying muzzle stands over him, chewing on something. The child's chin is mostly missing. People are peering out through the flaps of their tents, but no one comes to the child's rescue.

The two boys come running up. The older stoops to pick up a rock, which he hurls at the dog, missing, though the dog backs warily away from the child now.

> OLDER BOY
> (on his knees, quietly)
> Elvis.

ON THE CHILD. He's in shock now, not crying any more. The older boy starts to touch him, but stops, afraid. WE HOLD ON HIM until his terrified expression morphs into a mask of rage.

EXT. CAMP - SAME

ON THE RED DOG, running now, weaving among the tents. The older boy is chasing him, though the dog's nearly as big as he is. People have come out of their tents to watch. The boy picks up a rock and hurls it, missing.

EXT. OUTSKIRTS OF THE CAMP - SAME


The dog is running up a hill, at the top of which he stops, panting. A rock hits the animal in the ribs; it yelps and goes down. We see the boy approaching, another rock in his hand. The animal struggles to its feet, starts to limp off when the second rock hits him, and again the animal goes down. This time it lies still.

CLOSE ON THE BOY, as he approaches, exhausted. The dog is conscious, but makes no move to get to its feet. The boy picks up another larger stone. He drops to his knees before the panting dog, and as he raises it, we CUT TO:

EXT. CAMP - LATER

CLOSE ON THE BLUE BUCKET. The younger boy has carried it to the tent where he lives. People have gathered around him.
    The old boy walks up, still carrying the rock, now covered with blood. As is the boy himself, head to toe. He appears dazed, in a trance.


                    OLDER BOY'S VOICE
            This was when I was thirteen.


He kneels down next to the bucket. We see his reflection on the surface of the water. A drop of the dog's blood turns the water pink.

                OLDER BOY'S VOICE (CONT'D)
            He died too fast, that dog. I didn't want him dead.
            I wanted him dead-dead.


FROM ABOVE NOW, as the people form a circle around the boy, who continues to stare into the bucket.

ALI MOHAMED, Hyenas
ELIZABETH GILBERT, Cheekbone

AMIRA AL SAMMRAI, Breathing in the Rain
RICHARD BLANCO, Burning in the Rain

CHRISTINA MURRAY, Carrots
JONATHAN LETHEM, Carrot-Spotting

COLIN SHEPARD, Wildernesses
BILL ROORBACH, Heat Rises

ELIAS NASRAT, The Fate of the Trees
BETSY SHOLL, That Leafless Tree

HASSAN JEYLANI, A Day in Three Worlds
CAMPBELL MCGRATH, Night and Day

JULIAN MAYORQUIN, Bottle Jacking
GEORGE SAUNDERS, Go to Jail, After Eight Times, Go Directly to Jail

RICHARD AKERA, I Started to Explain
RICHARD RUSSO, Drinking Water

**VASSILY MURANGIRA, Swimming to Safety**
**ANN BEATTIE, Drive-by Alligator**

JANET MATHIESON, A Sandwich/An Olive
ARI MEIL, Jammy Brightness

MAHAD HILOWLE, The Table
SUSAN CONLEY, The Table

DARCIE SERFES, The Bump
LILY KING, Summer

NOAH WILLIAMS, Hunting in the Deep Woods
LEWIS ROBINSON, When Dad Rode Past Me

MICHÉE RUNYAMBO, Two Teeth
MONICA WOOD, History Lesson

EMILY HOLLYDAY, Cantaloupe
GIBSON FAY-LEBLANC, Self-Portrait, with Dish Rag

MISSOURI ALICE WILLIAMS, A Little Secret
MELISSA COLEMAN, Goddess of Liberation

FADUMO ISSACK, Climbing Barefoot
JAED COFFIN, The Coconut Tree

GRACE WHITED, Box of Hope
DAVE EGGERS, Pull the Sled, Feed the Fire

AQILA SHARAFYAR, The Faithful Doves of My Father
SARA CORBETT, I Thought I Could Fix Things

ARUNA KENYI, The Photograph
MICHAEL PATERNITI, We Are Trying to Understand What Happened to You There

# Swimming to Safety

*Vassily Murangira*

The best time to cry is at night, when the lights are out, and even if you sniffle a little, nobody can hear you. If people know that you are crying, they start asking about it. Sometimes, you don't feel comfortable enough to tell them who you are.

People may wonder why I write these things. Two years ago I found myself alone. I wondered what would become of my future without my family. I had learned from my parents how to be a mature person, and from my brothers how to wrestle. I wished I could have stayed and continued sharing these things with my family. This did not happen. But this is not the story I want to tell because it reminds me of many unbearable memories. Instead, I will tell you about a time in Africa that makes me smile.

It takes place in Burundi, my country, where my friends and I lived in a lakeside town called Bujumbura. The town had a beach where a crowd of people was always swimming, drinking soda and beer in the beach bar, and sunbathing on the sand. It's called Saga Beach. Sometimes at the beachside hotel both tourists and Burundians danced to an outdoor DJ. Sometimes people played volleyball or soccer in the sand. On the hottest days, when it was more than thirty-five degrees Celsius, I traveled to the beach with my friends. It was only twenty minutes away from my house.

On the day of my story, when we finished putting on our bathing suits, we went to play in the water. My friend Thierry was very competitive and told everyone else that we should have a swimming race. We would see who swam the fastest from the shore to a rock sticking out of the water. Elijah, Olivier, Chrislain, and I—we were all about the same age—decided that this would be a fun idea to keep us fresh on a hot day.

To make it more interesting, I proposed that my friends and I would give 2,000 Fbu (which is about $4 U.S.) from our pockets. We would leave the money on the beach under our clothes, where it would be safe and dry. The winner would receive all the money as a prize.

Chrislain and Olivier, who were sitting on the sand like everyone else, immediately agreed because they thought they had a good chance to win the money. Elijah didn't agree. He grumpily told me that 2,000 Fbu was too much money. He pretended to be angry with me, firing out insults like "dirty thief," and accused me of turning a fun game into something more serious. He complained that Chrislain, Thierry, Olivier, and I could easily afford to gamble but he couldn't because his family had less money.

As a solution, we decided to let Elijah play without putting in the money. We still put in our own money because we wanted the competition to depend on it—to put in everyone else's mind that there was more at stake. This was how our games became more exciting. Just like Elijah said, the game had become more serious, but now it was seriously fun.

We all stood up from the sand and formed a line at the top of the beach. Thierry yelled "Go!" without counting. But we were all ready for that. All five of us sprinted down the sand and into the water, making five big splashes.

As soon as we hit the water, I knew I was going to lose. *I'm not a very good swimmer*, I thought, *but at least I'm not the worst*. Chrislain was the worst because he was really fat. He liked to eat—he was the one who always wanted to eat French fries and fish and chicken at the beach bar. At least I knew I would not come in last place.

Everyone swam the crawl stroke, even Chrislain. We were all in a straight line. After just a few minutes of swimming, Elijah took the lead because he was so fast and had a muscular body. I was skinnier than Elijah, and that's why I was a little bit slower.

While we were swimming on ahead, Chrislain just gave up and floated on top of the water. He waved for us to come back, but we were still racing. I didn't have the money on my mind because I knew I was going to lose, but I kept swimming behind my friends to encourage them to swim even faster.

Elijah won by two body lengths. Thierry came in second place. Olivier came in third. I was fourth. And the last, of course, was Chrislain, who didn't even finish.

When we finished, we stopped swimming and just floated out by the rock, catching our breath. All of a sudden, we heard Chrislain yelling to us, "Gustave! Gustave!"

Gustave was a massive Nile crocodile who was sixty-five years old and twenty feet long. He was famous for being the biggest crocodile in Africa, and sometimes he made his home in Lake Tanganyika, our lake, when he was not in the Nile, Congo, or Zimbabwe.

I was scared for my life. I did not want to be eaten. We took Chrislain only half seriously, because he liked to joke around. But we headed out in the water, *fast*. People say that Gustave is a notorious man-eater because he has eaten over 300 people on the shores of Lake Tanganyika, and Lake Risizi in Rwanda. The last time Gustave had been seen was February 2008, and in our lake. He might still have been there.

All four of us screamed when we heard the name Gustave. We swam even faster than in the competition to get back to shore. Chrislain was waiting for us there, and he was screaming, too. I didn't know why I was swimming so fast because it probably wasn't true, but I wanted to save my life just in case. It was hard to breathe.

When we got to shore, we turned around, and saw that there was no Gustave behind us. Chrislain was laughing. We surrounded him while he was still laughing in the sand, and we tackled him. He told us to forgive him, and he promised he would not play those kinds of games again, because he could have made us drown with all of our fear. We forgave him, and then we showered and got dressed.

Elijah, who didn't even put in any money, received his prize. Before we left, Chrislain tried to get Elijah to buy him something to eat at the bar, but Elijah refused. He had a plan for his money. We all walked home together.

This is my last happy memory I have of my friends. Now I do not hear from them, but I hope that God will protect them. I hope they're still together as friends. A few days after this, my life was threatened and I had to escape Burundi to save it. I'm now living in Portland, Maine. Whatever happens on the earth, I won't be stressed, because God has the solutions. But I wonder if I will still be myself when everything is over.

# Drive-by Alligator

*Ann Beattie*

Two friends, let's call them Frou and B., met, as they often did, to take a little vacation and to get some sun and to get away from ordinary life and to laugh together, since they were old friends and they had a lot to laugh about, many years having passed and many different perspectives having been thrust upon them, like greatness. Then B. got a cold on his first day at the hotel, and Frou was left with the rental car and with very little compassion (she was a terrible person who felt—still feels—that colds are personal failings that can be avoided, even though she does not think this way when she gets a cold). Before this, though, on the half day before B. became ill, Frou paid the toll and the rental car whizzed across the bridge onto Sanibel and they headed to some nature refuge where they saw what was to be called, ever after, "drive-by alligator."

It was by a little pool of water—muddy water—behind a fence, and it paid no attention to the cars driving by, though when it was later imitated by Frou or by B., it rolled its eyes heavenward every now and then. Both people in the car identified: yes, it was an alligator, but it also sought sun and, probably, a break from being an alligator. People drove by and squealed, taking pictures and otherwise acting like silly tourists. They saw no nobility in the alligator. It was a prop. A cliché. The entire area in which it lived could have been a painted backdrop, the plants were so recognizable, the sky above so familiarly a blue Florida sky with white clouds like spun cotton candy.

The people in the car pointed and smiled and thought how perfect it was, the presence of an alligator, just when John Lennon's "Imagine" began playing on the radio. "Imagine there's no alligator," B. had begun to sing, even though he had a truly terrible voice that had never improved, in spite of years spent in the audience at Broadway musicals. They'd flown from two separate cities, converged at the sprawling hotel, the day was theirs, and right away, easy as could be, they saw some wildlife, instantly designated "drive-by alligator." Though Frou would like to give herself all the good lines, B. might very well have come up with that. Let's say he did.

Frou always drove because B. was quite overweight, never comfortable behind the wheel. He preferred the passenger seat, where he sat like Humpty Dumpty on the wall, even though we're talking leather seats and a soundtrack that could be changed as he wished, and of course he never toppled, he never broke.

Until he did. Years later, after the botched but briefly amusing Florida trip had passed into legend, into shorthand, into sound bites the two of them chuckled about on the phone, Frou was on a long trip and when she returned, she called B. and there was no answer, there was never an answer. She left messages, but as the reader will already realize, though she was too fearful to think it for a long time, he was dead. He had gone into a coma and died. The funeral had already taken place. She figured out where she had been that day, on what street, in what unfamiliar town, having no idea, of course no idea, because that idea was so unthinkable. There was probably some silly postcard still in the mail, on its way from Scotland to Bethesda, Maryland. But she'd never see him again, or the lit cabinets in his office filled with Star Wars figures, or his collection of globes, or his leather Chesterfield sofa, where for years she had lounged like an alligator, herself, telling B. everything she thought important, rolling her own eyes heavenward at some anecdote or some impossible question. At least, there were many things she thought important at the time, things the two of them always knew might one day be laughed over.

What if this was all invented, all made up? What if there were no such people—not many knew their nicknames; No, people would say, don't know that duo, but even if they existed, what is the *meaning* of the story of the alligator in Florida for everyone else, how does its larger significance waft off like a white cloud in a blue sky to make an intriguing Rorschach blot whose interpretation will of course never be wrong and never be right? Or: how does that cloud-finger spark the body of another, like God's famous finger on the ceiling of the Sistine Chapel? Because, really, you might as well gaze upward— for meaning; for a bemused eye roll; for the larger perspective. Otherwise, at ground level, there's nothing but an alligator, a creature sunning itself, doing nothing noteworthy, just lying there in its alligator way, with a shape as recognizable as a cookie cutter (Why not? You can buy a cactus cookie cutter; a fireplug cookie cutter; a dog-with-its-leg-lifted cookie cutter), doing nothing more than being the creature it is, on the day you see it (whether or not you see it). It means you no harm if you stay out of its way.

Heard that one before? Believe it?

It's hard to believe that it isn't waiting. That it isn't the image of mortality, glimpsed when least expected, in an unusual form, and that a person would be very silly, indeed, to feel that in naming it, he or she would remain safe. Of course, there was also the safety of the rental car. A red car wouldn't upset an alligator. It wasn't a bull, and anyway, this was Sanibel, not Pamplona.

ALI MOHAMED, Hyenas
ELIZABETH GILBERT, Cheekbone

AMIRA AL SAMMRAI, Breathing in the Rain
RICHARD BLANCO, Burning in the Rain

CHRISTINA MURRAY, Carrots
JONATHAN LETHEM, Carrot-Spotting

COLIN SHEPARD, Wildernesses
BILL ROORBACH, Heat Rises

ELIAS NASRAT, The Fate of the Trees
BETSY SHOLL, That Leafless Tree

HASSAN JEYLANI, A Day in Three Worlds
CAMPBELL MCGRATH, Night and Day

JULIAN MAYORQUIN, Bottle Jacking
GEORGE SAUNDERS, Go to Jail, After Eight Times, Go Directly to Jail

RICHARD AKERA, I Started to Explain
RICHARD RUSSO, Drinking Water

VASSILY MURANGIRA, Swimming to Safety
ANN BEATTIE, Drive-by Alligator

## JANET MATHIESON, A Sandwich/An Olive
## ARI MEIL, Jammy Brightness

MAHAD HILOWLE, The Table
SUSAN CONLEY, The Table

DARCIE SERFES, The Bump
LILY KING, Summer

NOAH WILLIAMS, Hunting in the Deep Woods
LEWIS ROBINSON, When Dad Rode Past Me

MICHÉE RUNYAMBO, Two Teeth
MONICA WOOD, History Lesson

EMILY HOLLYDAY, Cantaloupe
GIBSON FAY-LEBLANC, Self-Portrait, with Dish Rag

MISSOURI ALICE WILLIAMS, A Little Secret
MELISSA COLEMAN, Goddess of Liberation

FADUMO ISSACK, Climbing Barefoot
JAED COFFIN, The Coconut Tree

GRACE WHITED, Box of Hope
DAVE EGGERS, Pull the Sled, Feed the Fire

AQILA SHARAFYAR, The Faithful Doves of My Father
SARA CORBETT, I Thought I Could Fix Things

ARUNA KENYI, The Photograph
MICHAEL PATERNITI, We Are Trying to Understand What Happened to You There

# A Sandwich

*Janet Mathieson*

When I am home
I like to visit my one happy tree
& crawl up in its branches
with a sandwich that grins as wide as I do.

At the bottom my grubby hands
reach into the roots & pull up the dirt
& move inside the tree,
a strong tree, a living tree,
a body branching into our community,
an apple tree, a taste I remember.

When I am there
I imagine a little apartment
in the center of time
where my summer has just begun.
Where sunlight lasts forever
on that overhanging porch
& inside we eat bowls of bread & other treats,
& though I don't always like the meals
I love the people with whom I eat.

I imagine knives on a wooden cutting board,
someone hollering for salt,
little feet running to the table,
brownies in the oven,
herbs cooking on the stove,
warm cinnamon apple yams in the oven, so hot.
"Mmm, what'cha got, Mama?"

I'm a hop-along traveler.
The world is my home
& everywhere I go
there is a new person who cooks.
My favorite cook has glasses & spiky hair,
& the meanest spicy food bites my tongue
when he prepares
my wicked sandwich.

# An Olive

Smells like an oven in a decrepit house,
canned foods,
pickled foods
stored on its shelves.
But there's something bittersweet
about that smell.

A red purple color bleeding,
leaking onto everything it touches.
A tie-dyed pizza.
Contamination.
A hard rubber outside that is delicate
to touch & breaks
to spew the juices of some rotting creature inside.

It's like mud, silty mud,
not that gritty kind.
Almost gentle.

So powerful, so strong, so overwhelming.
It knocks my tongue out with that accidental
slip of the teeth
on its tender flesh.
It's not bitter, sweet, sour, or spicy.
It is a solitary creature
that fills your mouth with its toxic debris.

It tastes like the bottom of a pond.

# Jammy Brightness

*Ari Meil*

In my last life, I was a bike messenger in Shenyang, China. It was, for much of it, a tough life, stranded in bare dirty rooms below other bare dirty rooms. My good parents were ground to glass by the time I was old enough to know them. In all of the lives I've lived, I can't remember being so hungry while surrounded by so much. Still, swinging my rickety fixed-gear bike through the intense traffic of Shenyang during what seemed to be a constant rush hour was a thrill.

Here is something you should know about the seemingly immutable me that exists no matter who I am: I am able to experience absolute glee in certain moments, no matter how bad things get.

It was in one of those moments, thankfully, maybe not, swerving through thousands of moving obstacles, people, animals, lorries, that I ended that difficult life. Probably hit by a truck. It's pretty unusual to remember the few moments before death. There tends to be a lot of trauma. Though I vaguely remember, long ago, when I was a lonely mystic who spent his life wandering in some empty land, I sat down, an old man, and simply watched myself die. But the fact is that when you die, or at least, when I do, it doesn't matter what type of life or death you've had. It is always the same after that.

There is a feeling of loss like having duct tape ripped off your mouth then discovering that you still can't speak. Then comes the agony of memory: remembering all of the wonderful and horrible moments of a life. When your body is returned to the earth, there is a letting go, a relinquishing of what you did and didn't do in the past, and the shedding of that bodily cocoon. After that there is relief, followed immediately by an intense hunger—like you haven't eaten in a month.

Surrounded by earth with nothing on my mind but eating one of the huge sandwiches my uncle always makes me when I return home to my one happy tree, I crawl desperately through the soil, digging my way in the darkness until I feel it: a root that has reached down through space, through the various levels of reality and dreams, through time itself to guide me back to the center. And once I've felt it I know that I am on my way back home. I pull my hands through the dirt, guided by the loving curves of that ever-twining, powerful-reaching tendril until I emerge at the base of the tree. The tree at the center of time. My home.

Halfway up her gnarled trunk my family waits, in a sunny room that's been there so long it has grown into the tree itself, all windows and wood and branches.

I call her *my* one happy tree, but she has existed long before me, and will continue to *be* long, long after (though none of my family in this world has ever died, so I don't know what happens when one of us does). Her wrinkled striated bark climbs to heights beyond even my copious imagination, through the clouds and higher. Some of my brothers have tried climbing to the top, but none has ever even glimpsed her upper branches.

The rest of the lush evergreen wood that surrounds her, out past the curvature of whatever world this is, looks like miniatures in comparison. Oh, and one other thing: My tree is an olive tree, and she produces the most exquisite bitter, jubilant fruit that you have ever tasted, in this life or the next or the hundred or thousand before.

* * *

I'm sitting at our long, blond wooden table pondering the vast sandwich on the plate in front of me. It can seat over forty. The table, not the sandwich, but the sandwich could probably feed near that number back in Shenyang.

I'm so hungry that I am empty inside, just a roaring vacuum clamoring to be filled. But before I bite, I savor the dappled soft sunlight streaming through the wall of windows that is the curved wall of my home. I smell the sweet scented forest air pouring in. A few months ago I wouldn't have taken the time for this moment, but in my last few lives things have gotten complicated. And they have complicated this life too.

"Honey, aren't you going to eat?" my mother asks, a bit too worried about me since I've returned.

"Mmm," is all I give in response. Someone is always cooking in this house, and at this moment it is my mother. She is making cookies. She is thinking of me.

"Was it a hard month?" she asks gently.

This is how we talk about our lives, because no matter how long the life on earth, no matter what kind or quality of life it is, every human life takes one of our months to live. I have lived to be over 100 and I have died a baby, moments after birth. The time is the same, we say, because every life is of equal value.

When I abstained from eating the sandwich my uncle had made me, it was not to talk about feelings with my mom, so I reach down and grab a giant half, tomato and mayo oozing together down my hand and onto my wrist, fresh, just-roasted turkey and shiny algae-green lettuce shimmering from inside the rough-cut, thick-crusted bread, and I open my mouth as wide as it can stretch. The bite explodes into my mouth with the flavor of the tomato, its acidic jammy brightness shocking my tongue first, followed quickly by the mountainous depth of the turkey mellowing it out, using its flavor to flavor itself.

It is heaven, and I do not stop consuming it until there are only crumbs left on my plate.

"Have you thought about what we talked about before you . . . abruptly left last month?" my mother asks.

She had the decency to wait until I finished eating, which may have only taken a few moments, it's hard for me to say, it sort of felt like a hurricane in my mouth that raged until it passed.

"Let me rest, Mom, before we begin this argument again," I say, knowing that she has been nothing but kind to me and that the issue she is referring to is one of my own making. Though not exactly my choice.

I walk out of the room, our giant family's common room, and down the wooden path that winds one thousand feet above the ground to my room, which is really just a heavy platform nestled in the elbow of a twenty-foot-wide branch. I flop down on my bed like a toppling stack of empty boxes; a pile of wet dishes built too high.

When I wake it is evening and there is a warm buzz in my body. I have been dreaming.

Dreaming of him.

* * *

When I walk back into our communal room, my grandmother is brining olives from my tree, as she always is. Dusk is just transitioning into night, and the canopy of black-blue sky above us is rimmed with a spectrum of vibrant dark colors sliding into white at the horizon. I pull my stool up so that I'm facing her across the long counter and watch her deftly do a job that she has done since before the birth of Christ.

"You must eat," she says roughly as she works unperturbed in the boiling steam.

"I've eaten, Nana," I say, not minding her needling the way I do my mother's.

"You tried to find him?" she asks, not looking up from her work.

"No," I lie. Love is complicated when you live forever, long-distant cousins marrying cousins in your world, but falling in love again and again in the other.

"You did, I know. And it led to heartache as it must?"

The look she gives me is tender despite her tone.

"I didn't live long enough to make contact," I say, thinking of the small box I had addressed to him and strapped so carefully onto my bike the morning I set off into the streets to die. Again.

"That is for the best," she says. But something tells me that she doesn't entirely mean it.

Maybe it is because she wishes that I could change something she couldn't?

There is a family legend that when she was young, my grandmother tried to track down her love from a previous life, like I just did. No one is brave enough to ask her what happened, but whatever it was left her here, unwilling to return to that world, unmarried, brining olives for millennia.

"What was he like, Nana?" I ask. She just smiles into the steam.

"He was a small dark man," she says. "A shepherd who rarely laughed.

Back then we didn't choose our mates so the chances for love were less. I remember feeling as though I could not tell where he ended and I began."

Night outside the tall windows is still, light from the common room and platform bedrooms casting complicated shadows across rough, elephant-thick branches. In those shadows I see a lifetime of nights we spent together. He and I. Years of moments scattered across a continuum of silence, murmuring, talking, arguing, fighting, shouting, screaming. I had only made it to thirty-six, and of those years I spent eighteen with him. Half of a life.

Nana picks up nine finished jars and walks them to the pantry where they'll cool. I pick up one of the raw, unbrined olives and consider it hard.

These are our conduits to each life, these olives from my tree.

When I was a kid, we ate our olives and when enough time had passed we just dropped off the side of a platform like jumping in a lake. "Hold your nose and hop off."

The sensation of falling was terrifying and addictive.

I think I was eight when I first climbed as high as I could and then got a running start the entire length of a branch before leaping off, arms outstretched, careening through the summer air like a falcon, plunging for what seemed like an eternity toward the ground, toward absolute and imminent life.

That feeling of flying, the briny taste of olive still in my mouth, *so powerful, so strong, so overwhelming it knocks my tongue out with that accidental slip of the teeth on its tender flesh*, is me. No matter how much my heart breaks without him, I could never give up the exhilaration of leaping into life.

"Nana, do you believe the stories about what would happen if a mortal ate an olive?" I ask.

It is at this moment that my mother walks into the kitchen, and Nana uses the distraction to avoid my question.

There are ancient stories written in the old languages in the caverns of my tree. Some tell of our people bringing the olives to the other world. They say that if you give a mortal an olive, he can follow you here and become like one of us. My family dismisses the idea as impossible, because how could you get the olive to the other world? You obviously can't take it with you when you're born.

My mother walks over and tenderly hugs me. I am ashamed to admit it feels good.

"How are you doing?" she asks, too much concern in her voice.

"Great," I say without reciprocating her hug or even looking at her. This chastens her for a moment, and she busies herself getting ingredients from cupboards, no doubt preparing something wonderful for me to eat.

In a few moments, her frenzied movement subsides and she stands so still, as though her battery has run out.

"Honey, I just want you to know that I am not mad at you for running back to Earth. I know that you loved that man, and I get it that you wanted to go back and try and be with him again, but that never works. The thing to do is to take a break, like I asked you to.

"We've all had this happen, and it's hard, but eventually you get over it, and then you move on."

My anger isn't just because she's my mother, and she knows she is right, but because she is so damn sure that things have to be the way things always are. That drives me crazy. She has lived hundreds of lives, experienced so much of what there is to experience, and yet here she stands, telling me that this is just the way it is, this is our life. Move on. Get over it.

"Nana didn't just move on," I say, knowing at once that I should not have.

Both women look at me the way billions of stunned and offended mothers and grandmothers have looked at daughters when they have gone too far.

What I do next is so typical that I am a bit embarrassed, but it works.

I storm out of the room.

In the rich darkness of the night I climb big branches up, up, and farther up my tree, seeking someplace to cry alone. Before long I find myself in the same cavern where I'd cried myself out when I returned from my month with him.

It is the same deep nook where I decided I wouldn't just get over it the first time. It is where I rashly decided to return, and ended up in Shenyang. And where I broke the rules and figured out how to get an olive to the mortal world.

\* \* \*

When I wake again it is morning. There's a wicked crick in my neck from sleeping propped against the smooth walls of the tree. I climb out of the cavern, fingers touching nicks and carvings left there long ago, and look out on the distant curvature of the world. The sun is shining down on the forest floor far below, dew gone, the dusty light of late morning curling through the low branches. Refreshed somehow, at peace, I begin my descent.

In the great communal room at the center of time, in the heart of my one happy tree, everyone is eating. I close my eyes and listen to the *knives on wooden cutting boards, someone hollering for salt, little feet running to the table.*

As I smile I think of him, of the little box with the olive from my tree, addressed, every ounce of my heart poured into a note that tries to explain what I remembered when that gorgeous pigeon delivered a magic gift to my balcony in Shenyang.

I imagine the package lying on the sidewalk by my body, a bit crumpled. I consider the idea that someone may have picked it up and mailed it, and I know that if it was meant to be, it would be.

From across the room my mother smiles, and despite my instincts, I smile back.

There is an empty place at the table between my brothers, who are bickering, and when I take it they give me rough hugs and continue on as though nothing has changed.

ALI MOHAMED, Hyenas
ELIZABETH GILBERT, Cheekbone

AMIRA AL SAMMRAI, Breathing in the Rain
RICHARD BLANCO, Burning in the Rain

CHRISTINA MURRAY, Carrots
JONATHAN LETHEM, Carrot-Spotting

COLIN SHEPARD, Wildernesses
BILL ROORBACH, Heat Rises

ELIAS NASRAT, The Fate of the Trees
BETSY SHOLL, That Leafless Tree

HASSAN JEYLANI, A Day in Three Worlds
CAMPBELL MCGRATH, Night and Day

JULIAN MAYORQUIN, Bottle Jacking
GEORGE SAUNDERS, Go to Jail, After Eight Times, Go Directly to Jail

RICHARD AKERA, I Started to Explain
RICHARD RUSSO, Drinking Water

VASSILY MURANGIRA, Swimming to Safety
ANN BEATTIE, Drive-by Alligator

JANET MATHIESON, A Sandwich/An Olive
ARI MEIL, Jammy Brightness

## MAHAD HILOWLE, The Table
## SUSAN CONLEY, The Table

DARCIE SERFES, The Bump
LILY KING, Summer

NOAH WILLIAMS, Hunting in the Deep Woods
LEWIS ROBINSON, When Dad Rode Past Me

MICHÉE RUNYAMBO, Two Teeth
MONICA WOOD, History Lesson

EMILY HOLLYDAY, Cantaloupe
GIBSON FAY-LEBLANC, Self-Portrait, with Dish Rag

MISSOURI ALICE WILLIAMS, A Little Secret
MELISSA COLEMAN, Goddess of Liberation

FADUMO ISSACK, Climbing Barefoot
JAED COFFIN, The Coconut Tree

GRACE WHITED, Box of Hope
DAVE EGGERS, Pull the Sled, Feed the Fire

AQILA SHARAFYAR, The Faithful Doves of My Father
SARA CORBETT, I Thought I Could Fix Things

ARUNA KENYI, The Photograph
MICHAEL PATERNITI, We Are Trying to Understand What Happened to You There

# The Table

*Mahad Hilowle*

My parents were really young when they met, young still when they got married and made me. I am the oldest, Mahad, *like gold*. We lived the hard way because my father, Said, *helpful,* kept losing jobs. He was a building contractor, but it was hard to find a job in Somalia. I remember how my mother, Fadumo, *mother of nature,* used to cook flatbread and soup with chicken, and give me lemon tea with sugar when I was sick. We had no table; it is the tradition there to sit on the floor and eat.

My mother and little brother were not home on the day the rebels came to our home. I was in my room studying when I heard a loud crack. I went out into the living room and saw the door broken down, and my father bleeding from his head. My sisters and brothers were all in the living room surrounded by large men with weapons. I wanted to scream, but I couldn't make any sound. My heart dropped. My brothers, Faisal, *prince*, Fahad, *king*, and sisters, Ilhan, *star*, Faiso, *hero*, and Fardowsa, *heaven,* were crying for help. The rebels took money, my mother's jewelry, and anything of value before a violent leave-taking. We all felt so lost and lonely. We went to my grandfather's house where he arranged for us to go to Egypt. We fled for our lives, losing my mother and little brother Abdulah, *son of God*, in Somalia.

We lived in Cairo for four years. My father worked all the time, all the time. As a mechanic, in housekeeping—whatever it took to feed the family. We were in a rough neighborhood in Cairo, but our apartment was fully furnished; we had television, beds, a washing machine. My mother and little brother were still lost in the Somali civil war, but a family friend from Somalia, Shokre, *sweet,* took care of my little sisters, while the rest of us went to school. We were safe. In Cairo, I remember eating a lot of beets, and beans, and sometimes rice with beef, just grabbing food and eating alone. We had a round kitchen table with a mirror tabletop. My family never ate together.

It was seven years of running before my mother caught up with us here in Portland, and my brother Abdulah is in Ethiopia with my aunt, but he will come to America next month. I have a new baby brother here, Jihan, *paradise*. Now, we have a long wooden table with a stone top with eight tall chairs—enough for everybody. For dinner we eat pasta and tomato sauce with meatballs. We drink soda or juice, and my little sisters drink milk. I am the oldest and sit next to my father. My three sisters and two brothers line the sides of the table. They respect me and never sit at the right, next to my father. My father sits at one end of our long, solid table and my mother at the other end like the bookends of our family story.

# The Table

*Susan Conley*

Our kitchen table was round. It came from a maple tree in the woods out back that was cut and planked and sanded by a friend up the river—a man who'd left mathematics.

My parents were really young when they met, and it was the first piece of furniture they owned. In 1972 the Army discharged my father from Fort Knox in Tennessee because of wobbly ankles. He went back to Maine where he'd been raised. Woolwich was a place for farmers and shipbuilders and now the back to the landers and the war protesters.

Our house stood at the top of a long, sloping field. Wild turkeys roamed the woods and always the deer. For a while we raised sheep, and that was exciting until it was time to eat them.

Here are the things that mattered to me: the forest because of the hideouts, the river because of the mudflats that sucked you in like quicksand and how great was that and how scary, and the table.

The wood was soft. You could engrave your name on it with a steak knife or a fork tine when Mom wasn't looking: I WAS HERE. SC loves DH.

There was just enough room for the four of us. I was the oldest. My brother liked the meats: pot roast and pork loin and steak. I had to pretend to like the meats.

Then we had a baby sister and there was just enough room for the five of us. We ate spaghetti in a tomato sauce with bay leaves that my mother simmered on the burner all day. We ate drumsticks fried in the most delicious batter and stacked on a paper towel to cool. We weren't religious on Sundays, but we ate early that day, and we ate roast beef.

We always ate together. The table had four legs and it was high enough to scoot your chair underneath and not bang your knees. The seats were made of a kind of rope that itched.

Please finish your meal.

You're not getting up till you clean your plate.

This could take time. Where was the dog when you needed her? Where was the napkin you'd dropped on the floor? The trick was to get the gristle from the plate to your hand to your dog.

Please pass the salt.

Please pass the butter.

Can I have some more milk?

Can I have a ride to the YMCA?

I don't remember anything else we said.

The table has now taken on the features of my brother. He's tall and dark-haired and how can that be? That I see the table and I see my brother? Then I see my sister and my father and mother. The table is like a family. Like a beating heart.

ALI MOHAMED, Hyenas
ELIZABETH GILBERT, Cheekbone

AMIRA AL SAMMRAI, Breathing in the Rain
RICHARD BLANCO, Burning in the Rain

CHRISTINA MURRAY, Carrots
JONATHAN LETHEM, Carrot-Spotting

COLIN SHEPARD, Wildernesses
BILL ROORBACH, Heat Rises

ELIAS NASRAT, The Fate of the Trees
BETSY SHOLL, That Leafless Tree

HASSAN JEYLANI, A Day in Three Worlds
CAMPBELL MCGRATH, Night and Day

JULIAN MAYORQUIN, Bottle Jacking
GEORGE SAUNDERS, Go to Jail, After Eight Times, Go Directly to Jail

RICHARD AKERA, I Started to Explain
RICHARD RUSSO, Drinking Water

VASSILY MURANGIRA, Swimming to Safety
ANN BEATTIE, Drive-by Alligator

JANET MATHIESON, A Sandwich/An Olive
ARI MEIL, Jammy Brightness

MAHAD HILOWLE, The Table
SUSAN CONLEY, The Table

## DARCIE SERFES, The Bump
## LILY KING, Summer

NOAH WILLIAMS, Hunting in the Deep Woods
LEWIS ROBINSON, When Dad Rode Past Me

MICHÉE RUNYAMBO, Two Teeth
MONICA WOOD, History Lesson

EMILY HOLLYDAY, Cantaloupe
GIBSON FAY-LEBLANC, Self-Portrait, with Dish Rag

MISSOURI ALICE WILLIAMS, A Little Secret
MELISSA COLEMAN, Goddess of Liberation

FADUMO ISSACK, Climbing Barefoot
JAED COFFIN, The Coconut Tree

GRACE WHITED, Box of Hope
DAVE EGGERS, Pull the Sled, Feed the Fire

AQILA SHARAFYAR, The Faithful Doves of My Father
SARA CORBETT, I Thought I Could Fix Things

ARUNA KENYI, The Photograph
MICHAEL PATERNITI, We Are Trying to Understand What Happened to You There

# The Bump

*Darcie Serfes*

Life was simple before motherhood bumped into me.
I am unable to put back together the broken pieces of my dreams; finish high school, go to college.

I am going to be a mother.
I am anxious, depressed, scared, trapped in a tunnel.
I hide behind a smiling face.
It's going to get worse before it gets better.
Be strong.
My baby can sense it.
Instinct is running through my body.

Cocoa butter doesn't work.
At seventeen, my body is not supposed to look like this; stretch marks on my breasts, my thighs, my belly.
When I look at my body in the mirror it looks like a tiger attacked it.

I wish Madison came after I got my life straight; was a college graduate, had a good paying job.
At the same time I don't think I would be in school if I had not gotten pregnant.
I would be doing drugs.
Hanging out with the wrong people.

My mom went through all of this.
I would be lost without her.
She is thirty-five and already a grandma.

Both my grandma and mother are overwhelmed, but happy.
My grandmother prays and belly dances in the living room.
My mother tells me, "You opened your legs, now you have a baby. I raised four kids. This is your responsibility."

I went into labor during the night and didn't want to wake anyone.
I took showers and swayed my hips through the contractions.
By morning I couldn't wait.
The ambulance came.
The men told me not to push but I couldn't help it.
We got to the hospital ten minutes before Madison Emilia.

I miss the feeling of being pregnant.
I love telling people about birth.
It's a pain only a mother can understand, and I survived it.
Room service at the hospital was great.
I had brownies with cherries, French fries, and pickles.

Now that Madison is out, I can't protect her.
I could when she was in my belly.
I am scared of Madison dying.
I had a dream my baby turned into a gremlin and attacked me.
What if something happens when I am not there?

My sister taught me to use my mouth to suck the snot out of my baby's nose.
It works, but I can't do it.
My baby wails when you dress her, and she curls her lip when she poops.
I hate waking up in the middle of the night with Madison, but I could not sleep without her near.

I am fucking up a little.
It's hard to focus on schoolwork.
I don't know what I will do now.
Maybe I will be a midwife.

I want to say it was a mistake getting pregnant so young, but it wasn't.

# Summer

*Lily King*

She opened her legs and now in the hallways she looks at me like my mother always does like I should've known the future like she's so disappointed she can't even speak. I can't even speak to you my mother will say her big hand blocking me out and the smallness inside getting a little smaller.

\* \* \*

And then she's gone from school and the other girls are talking and I don't ask what and it's weird not having to avoid her not seeing that belly cresting around a corner then the rest of her trailing behind.

\* \* \*

Some days I've nearly forgotten and it was one of those days. A summer day. It's the legs I see first thrashing bare and fat caught in a little pouch that crisscrosses across her back. I know the slope of the back of her head. The kid's screaming shrill as a knife. The other register opens up and I put the beers on the counter. I wait for her to notice. We're three feet apart and my heart's beating hard like it used to for her and I barely hear the old man say five-nineteen. I slide the cash over silently and figure I've got a few seconds before she catches me. But she doesn't look over. She leaves. And through the window she bends with the weight of her bags the weight of that writhing kid. I keep looking the beers cold in my hands and she presses her lips to the top of her baby's head the soft part that's dented in a bit like a bruise on a peach as if that kid were cute and sound asleep as if she were deaf to the hollering and numb to the kicking as if that baby would never do wrong no matter how many mistakes. I don't think nobody will ever kiss me like that. She lifts her head slides her pinky in the baby's mouth and they're gone.

# Hunting in the Deep Woods

*Noah Williams*

In Maine, there is an old adage: If you don't like the weather, wait five minutes.

I've been waiting for three hours, and it's still freezing cold out here. It's so cold, in fact, that every time I exhale, a little puff of steam comes out of my mouth and floats down onto the gun cradled in my lap. It stains a small patch of the barrel black with condensation. I'm breathing through my mouth because it's quieter, or at least seems quieter, than when I breathe through my nose. Deer are sensitive about these things.

The tiny beads of water on my rifle have frozen into hard little droplets. This is where moisture comes to die. It's an old gun, with lots of dings, and nicks, and scratches to prove that this isn't its first day afield. My grandfather carried it with him for some sixty years before me, and it killed lots of deer. Old guns are always better for days like these, especially when your spit freezes before it hits the ground.

I've met lots of real Maine people during my sixteen years here. Not like the way a politician meets "real people," though. I know farmers and lobstermen, carpenters and heating techs, and lots and lots of teachers. Maine farmers do not wear overalls, chew straw, and smile as they drive by on their shiny green tractors. They are tough men, and even tougher women. They work longer and harder in a day than most people do in a week. Their tractors are not gleaming mounds of GPS-guided steel, but clunky old Olivers held together with baling twine and patch welds. Lobstermen and fishermen are equally tough, and maybe twice as hardy. They must run in sync with the weather, the tides, and work in blistering sun and bone-chilling fog.

Speaking of cold, the nine-hour hand-warmers have tapped out at four, and I'm starting to lose feeling in my fingers. My toes are long gone. As the sun comes up, the complete and utter silence changes to just plain silence. The movement of a small bird hopping through the pine tree overhead punctuates the nothingness.

To be a Mainer (and not the kind who descends in June and then beats a hasty retreat back to Florida come September) you have to be tough. You need this tolerance and stamina that I've yet to see anywhere else. It's not determined by race, or gender, occupation, or religion. The term "Mainer" is its own demographic group.

I pack it in. I can't take this any longer. Any exposed flesh on my body has gone from painfully cold to pleasantly warm and tingly. The sun creeps toward the treetops as I push through the dense grove of hemlocks, into scattered second-year beech cuts, and back onto the old logging road. As I come around the bend, another hunter hiking in waves to me.

"Any luck?" he says, huffing and puffing. I look at his fancy sunglasses, immaculate blaze-orange parka with a black camouflage print, the glittering rifle in his right hand, and then back to my beat-up old 30-30 and I think of the two pairs of pants I'm wearing. For a split second, I wish we could trade places.

"Nothing yet, but I'm hopeful," I say.

The man shivers. "Jesus, it's cold out. I'm glad I wasn't here any earlier."

I just smile, and am grateful for this morning, for the cold, and for this meeting. More than anything I'm grateful for the place I am right here and now.

# When Dad Rode Past Me

*Lewis Robinson*

Dad and I were looking for a way to spend some quality time together, and I suggested we enlist in the Trek Across Maine, a 300-mile bicycling expedition from the western mountains to the coast. Dad had never really logged hours on a bike and was a long-time smoker, but he was game. During the months leading up to the Trek, I would touch base with him periodically to see how he was doing with his training. Once when we were chatting on the phone at the end of a sunny weekend, he told me about an incredible ride he'd been on. Midway through the conversation, as he was describing the many towns he'd seen and the distances he'd covered, it dawned on me that he'd been out on his Harley.

His bicycle, an old Schwinn tank, was blanketed with dust in his basement. He didn't like that I was keeping tabs on his training. He said a few times, "We can just wing it, can't we?" And I would say no, and he would ask me how much we needed to train, and I would tell him "a lot," though I wasn't training either.

When the weekend of the Trek arrived, I convinced him to don some Lycra bike shorts and a bright-red bicycle jersey so that we could at least look like we'd trained.

I can still see Dad now: just ahead of me, starting up yet another incline during that first day, royal-blue bike helmet canted to the side, his skinny Lycra-clad ass, his freckled legs doggedly churning the pedals.

We reached our destination—Farmington—about six hours later than many of the other riders. It was 90 degrees out. The fastest Trekkers had sped through those first 100 miles to avoid frying on the asphalt in the middle of the day. Dad and I had inched up the steepest climbs at high noon. How slowly can you travel without falling over? Pretty slowly. The Lycra didn't save us.

Ten hours on a bike in the hot sun when you're not used to biking is not fun. But there we were, finally freewheeling into Farmington, the sun low in the sky. Zombie-like, we flitted past strip malls toward the center of town.

While we coasted, I thought about how great it would it have been to be sheathed in leather on Dad's Harley, rumbling into this mountain town looking for a good hamburger. I cursed our Lycra. This was not how Dad and I had ever experienced Maine together. We preferred Moody's Diner, the batting cage in Rockland, a high-school basketball game in a packed gym.

Still a few miles from the finish, we scanned the roadside for a good place to pee. There weren't many options. I spotted a construction equipment dealership and pulled in, Dad right behind me. The dirt lot was full of bulldozers and backhoes. Dad rolled right up to one of them, leaned his bike against it, and pulled down his Lycra. Propriety wanes when you're very, very tired.

The owner of the dealership saw us through the window of his repair shop, and he sprinted out into the lot to yell at us. "You people are assholes!" That was his opening line. It got much worse from there. I'm sure he'd been dealing with bike tourists all day.

My dad, a guy comfortable with heavy machinery—a man who prided himself on being able to talk to anyone, anywhere—pulled up his pants and did not respond.

I made the poor choice of pleading our case, and apologizing. I told the owner we'd had a really long day, and we weren't thinking straight. He said he was calling the cops. That's when I wanted to explain to him: we'd never worn Lycra shorts before. I wanted to take off our bike helmets, and our bike jerseys, and show the guy we were regular people. But all I could do was stammer, which made him yell even more. And jot down our bib numbers.

I was still talking when Dad rode past me; he'd mounted his bike and was back on the course.

* * *

Later, I should have apologized to Dad for this. For this, and for all of the other trials I put him through over the years. (When I was away in college, he received a warrant for my arrest in the mail. He forwarded it along to me with a handwritten note on the envelope, "Lew—what's up?")

Yes, I should have apologized, even though he wouldn't have wanted to hear it. He didn't want to sweat the small stuff. He was too busy being grateful for the time we had together.

ALI MOHAMED, Hyenas
ELIZABETH GILBERT, Cheekbone

AMIRA AL SAMMRAI, Breathing in the Rain
RICHARD BLANCO, Burning in the Rain

CHRISTINA MURRAY, Carrots
JONATHAN LETHEM, Carrot-Spotting

COLIN SHEPARD, Wildernesses
BILL ROORBACH, Heat Rises

ELIAS NASRAT, The Fate of the Trees
BETSY SHOLL, That Leafless Tree

HASSAN JEYLANI, A Day in Three Worlds
CAMPBELL MCGRATH, Night and Day

JULIAN MAYORQUIN, Bottle Jacking
GEORGE SAUNDERS, Go to Jail, After Eight Times, Go Directly to Jail

RICHARD AKERA, I Started to Explain
RICHARD RUSSO, Drinking Water

VASSILY MURANGIRA, Swimming to Safety
ANN BEATTIE, Drive-by Alligator

JANET MATHIESON, A Sandwich/An Olive
ARI MEIL, Jammy Brightness

MAHAD HILOWLE, The Table
SUSAN CONLEY, The Table

DARCIE SERFES, The Bump
LILY KING, Summer

NOAH WILLIAMS, Hunting in the Deep Woods
LEWIS ROBINSON, When Dad Rode Past Me

MICHÉE RUNYAMBO, Two Teeth
MONICA WOOD, History Lesson

EMILY HOLLYDAY, Cantaloupe
GIBSON FAY-LEBLANC, Self-Portrait, with Dish Rag

MISSOURI ALICE WILLIAMS, A Little Secret
MELISSA COLEMAN, Goddess of Liberation

FADUMO ISSACK, Climbing Barefoot
JAED COFFIN, The Coconut Tree

GRACE WHITED, Box of Hope
DAVE EGGERS, Pull the Sled, Feed the Fire

AQILA SHARAFYAR, The Faithful Doves of My Father
SARA CORBETT, I Thought I Could Fix Things

ARUNA KENYI, The Photograph
MICHAEL PATERNITI, We Are Trying to Understand What Happened to You There

# Two Teeth

*Michée Runyambo*

My neighborhood was so beautiful. I loved the quiet of the place, the mango trees, and the forest on the sides. Every house was a different color. Ours was red, and nothing ever happened in it without the others knowing about it. The streets were narrow and full of dirt. Whenever the sun was out you could hear the women singing; at night it was the drunk man's turn.

One morning there were no birds singing, and no kids were playing soccer in the street. The air was thick and cloudy, but day had finally come. We could actually see the damage of the lights in the sky, and hear the loud bangs on the streets and sharp sounds all around us. We could see where they hit. We could see that we were at war.

We were hiding in my uncle's house. Ours was too dangerous. It was too big, too noticeable, and they knew where my father lived. All eight of us were hiding in one room, trying to keep ourselves quiet and eating what we could find, which was mostly water and beans. There were only two beds, so some of us tried to sleep on the floor. The room was small. The walls were made out of mud over bricks, and the roof was made out of metal.

It rained that night. I always loved it when it rained. You could hear the drops, and that relaxed me. With everything that had happened—my father leaving, bullets flying all around us, and bombs exploding—rain seemed to decrease the fear. We sat there in that room together for hours not saying a word, just listening and hoping that the next bomb wouldn't fall on us. My little sister was five years old. I remember her crying that night and mom telling her it was okay. "God's with us," she said. She held her tight and you could see all the trouble leaving the little girl's face.

My mother is a brave woman. She took responsibility for keeping us safe.

As the rain fell down, I could hear my mother's voice, singing in the corner of the room. Her voice filled my head, and my eyes gave up. I started crying. It seemed as if the more she sang the calmer I became and the more I thought that this was just a nightmare. My little brother was lying next to me. He told me he couldn't stop his hands from shaking, so I held them and told him to sleep. "Everything will be okay tomorrow morning."

The joy in the room was found in my youngest sister. She was young and innocent and whenever bombs exploded, she clapped her hands and laughed. A plate of beans was in the middle of the room, and she struggled to crawl to the plate to eat. Minutes later the small room smelled like our neighborhood dump yard. My baby sister sat there laughing and through her smile you could see her only two teeth. The smell was so intolerable that we were tempted to get out, and even the bullets seemed better at that moment. We all sat there laughing together, and for a brief moment we forgot about the fear that was keeping us there.

# History Lesson

*Monica Wood*

I once loved the brick sidewalks and cobblestoned streets of Portland, Maine. I liked to close my eyes and imagine the murmuring of top-hatted entrepreneurs ambling across the square, the rustling skirts of a young matron pushing a pram, the zippering sound of awnings being opened for the day. Each brick and stone, I imagined, contained the life force of some long-dead resident of my historically rich city, the dust and heat of their footfalls embedded in the ground.

But on this sunny afternoon in the present day, strolling the Old Port with my sister Betty, those same cobbles and bricks seem willfully misaligned, hostile and frost-heaved: an exposed edge here, a divot there, myriad toeholds awaiting an unsuspecting toe. "Watch your step," I tell her every few seconds. "You have to keep an eye on those bricks."

"Keep an eye on those bricks," she vows, then forgets in an instant, too enamored of the cityscape: animals, musicians, babies, hot-dog stands.

"Look at that dog," she says. "What brand dog is that?"

"Pit bull, I think. Watch where you're going, Betty, okay?"

"That's a nice dog," she continues. "Handsome." The dog's owner—a tattooed heavyweight jangling with chains—shoots her a grin.

"What do you say we sit for a while, Bet?"

She nods. "That's a good opinion."

We cross Monument Square to rest at the massive foot of Our Lady of Victories, to take our bearings in a safe, untrippable spot. I feel the way I always do when my tiny, frail older sister comes to visit: physically gigantic; twitchy and vigilant.

"Aw, look at the tobblers," Betty says, spotting a daycare worker lugging a pack of kids in a cart, a twenty-first-century version of horse and buggy. Then she turns to me, her face awash in old light. "I pulled *you* in a wagon!"

I laugh. Indeed she did, in a time before my conscious memory.

She laughs, too; unlike other literal-minded souls, Betty appreciates irony. "I *pulled* you!"

We have the photograph to prove it: six-year-old Betty in a gingham dress and bare feet, towing an apple-red Radio Flyer in which my sister Cathy and I sit like piglets being hauled to a fair. In the picture she looks tall for her age, lean and leggy, a species apart from the chubby "tobblers" who have wheedled her into the ride that will turn into her earliest, and favorite, memory.

I love this memory, too, in part because it belongs to her alone. My own earliest memories also kick in around the age of six, which is to say I don't recall the wagon ride, nor a time of not knowing my "big" sister was different. I curl my arm around her rickety shoulders, explaining that the statue looming over us stands in memory of men killed in the Civil War. Was there ever a time when instead she explained things to me? Not civil war, no; but maybe how to properly pick up a kitten? How to sip a spoonful of Campbell's without spilling? Did she warn me to watch my step as I toddled headlong into our yard?

"I don't like war," she says. "Too violent."

I point skyward. "Impressive, though, isn't she?" At fourteen feet, Lady Victory is one big-boned gal.

"Wow," she agrees, feigning awe for my benefit. But to Betty, history is not larger than life. It is exactly human scale. It includes only the people and things she has personally loved. It spans sixty-three years. And, like all history, it is paved with facts but potholed with longing.

She's still thinking of the wagon. "You and Cathy were little," she informs me. "But I think I was a larger age."

When did I first know? Did I wake up one day at four, or five, and see all at once that she was less agile, more helpless, slower to comprehend? Is that how it happened, as an electrifying *thwack* of comprehension? Or was it a gradual knowing, like sitting on a beach and realizing the tide you've been watching has begun to recede before you registered its full height?

I look at her now: eighty pounds, fragile as a wren. "You'll always be a larger age, Bet," I tell her. "No matter how long we live."

It occurs to me then, as we chat in the shade of a century-old monument, that Betty will always have a "larger" memory, too. When I was one, two, three, she was the big girl already storing the facts of our joined life. "What was I like?" I ask her.

"Sweeet," she assures me. She puts enough *es* in "sweet" to frost a cake, smoothing the air with her bony hand. "You were a sweeet baby."

I happen to know, through other authorities, that I was in fact a tantrum-throwing growler, but I gladly choose her version. "What else?"

She tells me I wore a blue sunsuit, and then I see it, I think I see it: buttons, ruffles, a strap that keeps falling off my shoulder. She recalls a doll carriage, a toy bus, our darling father laughing.

Most people smile to see us chatting; one or two avert their eyes. They know how to tell time, count change, walk on malevolent bricks without tripping. Some, like me, can prune a hydrangea, sing in French, trim a cat's claws, write a book. Betty can do none of these things. But she is better than I— than everyone—at recalling her world through a mollifying cloud of sympathy. Who among us doesn't want to hear of our long-ago sweetness?

I get up and offer her a hand. "What do you say, Bet? Shall we hit the bricks?"

She's up in an instant. "Onward and awkward," she chirps, and here we go—*watch your step, Betty, watch your step*—shaping our own tiny story, adding our dust to the uneven cobbles of history.

ALI MOHAMED, Hyenas
ELIZABETH GILBERT, Cheekbone

AMIRA AL SAMMRAI, Breathing in the Rain
RICHARD BLANCO, Burning in the Rain

CHRISTINA MURRAY, Carrots
JONATHAN LETHEM, Carrot-Spotting

COLIN SHEPARD, Wildernesses
BILL ROORBACH, Heat Rises

ELIAS NASRAT, The Fate of the Trees
BETSY SHOLL, That Leafless Tree

HASSAN JEYLANI, A Day in Three Worlds
CAMPBELL MCGRATH, Night and Day

JULIAN MAYORQUIN, Bottle Jacking
GEORGE SAUNDERS, Go to Jail, After Eight Times, Go Directly to Jail

RICHARD AKERA, I Started to Explain
RICHARD RUSSO, Drinking Water

VASSILY MURANGIRA, Swimming to Safety
ANN BEATTIE, Drive-by Alligator

JANET MATHIESON, A Sandwich/An Olive
ARI MEIL, Jammy Brightness

MAHAD HILOWLE, The Table
SUSAN CONLEY, The Table

DARCIE SERFES, The Bump
LILY KING, Summer

NOAH WILLIAMS, Hunting in the Deep Woods
LEWIS ROBINSON, When Dad Rode Past Me

MICHÉE RUNYAMBO, Two Teeth
MONICA WOOD, History Lesson

**EMILY HOLLYDAY, Cantaloupe**
**GIBSON FAY-LEBLANC, Self-Portrait, with Dish Rag**

MISSOURI ALICE WILLIAMS, A Little Secret
MELISSA COLEMAN, Goddess of Liberation

FADUMO ISSACK, Climbing Barefoot
JAED COFFIN, The Coconut Tree

GRACE WHITED, Box of Hope
DAVE EGGERS, Pull the Sled, Feed the Fire

AQILA SHARAFYAR, The Faithful Doves of My Father
SARA CORBETT, I Thought I Could Fix Things

ARUNA KENYI, The Photograph
MICHAEL PATERNITI, We Are Trying to Understand What Happened to You There

# Cantaloupe

*Emily Hollyday*

Every day I wear my shiny red cowboy boots.
Sometimes I even wear them when I stand on my table.
I pretend I'm doing magic.
Sometimes I perform tintinnabulations.
The problem is my soles get real sticky.
No one cleans up their juice from their cantaloupe.

I always clean up my own cantaloupe!
In my house, there are lots of good bells for tintinnabulations.
Mom uses them to call us to the dinner table.
When she rings the bells I come running. My boots
help me run really fast, almost like magic.
Then I wash my hands because they're usually pretty sticky.

I don't mind being sticky.
It just means I've been playing hard in my boots.
I know how long I've been playing. Tintinnabulations
come from our church every hour. During Sunday school we feast on cantaloupe,
and guess what? We don't even eat it at a table.
We sit in a circle on the ground and talk about God and magic.

I don't really believe in magic.
I just like to eat that cantaloupe
while I admire my shiny red boots.
I shine them every day so they won't be sticky.
You know how I told you about how I perform tintinnabulations?
Well, Mom yells at me when she finds boot prints on her table.

She says that food is the only thing that should be on the table.
Here's the problem: food makes it really sticky—especially cantaloupe.
When I stand on the table I pretend I'm God, using all my magic.
Too bad God doesn't have red shiny cowboy boots.
He'd look pretty neat up in heaven listening to tintinnabulations!

I bet you don't even know what that word even means—*tintinnabulations*.
I swear it's not some sort of wacky magic.
It means the ringing of bells. Like on summer nights when it's hot and sticky,
the bells don't ring and I don't know when to go to the table,
and so instead I eat my cantaloupe
at the playground standing tall in my red boots.

All you need are some boots and a little magic.
Sometimes things get sticky, and that's when it's time to go home, stand on your table,
listen to some tintinnabulations, and eat some cantaloupe.

# Self-Portrait, with Dish Rag

*Gibson Fay-LeBlanc*

Some nights I slip on my brown leather boots
after dinner and announce to the table
I'm headed to a reading. I need magic
thumping in my chest, those tintinnabulations
in my inner ear. The table's probably sticky
because no one cleans up their cantaloupe.

I hate the boys' and wife's cantaloupe
after I've gone to hear those tintinnabulations
and come back later to that hand-me-down table
of wilting rinds and pools that drip on boots
that Emmett calls *writer boots* for their magic
that makes me taller even when they're sticky.

Fingerprints on white trim, wood floor sticky
with dried juice and pretzels crushed by boots
that didn't see them set off tintinnabulations
in my head. I want to control the cantaloupe.
I want unbroken windows, clear floors and table.
I want the house to sweep itself like magic.

I know a house can't sweep itself by magic.
The boys and wife all covet cantaloupe
and all admire me in my writer boots,
but everyone's too busy for a sticky
floor someone had better tintinnabulate
the hell out of, along with the table.

It might as well be me: a smooth table,
dining chairs not soiled, walls not sticky,
are all a way to tell the cantaloupe
we are okay, this family has magic,
and, look at me, under control, in boots,
making the house sparkle like tintinnabulations

while the others sleep through tintinnabulations
downstairs and dream of kid and doctor magic
which both involve making it all sticky
again. Nothing is more than this table,
where we four sit together with cantaloupes
and talk at night, often without my boots.

I know boots are not what holds the magic,
and my sticky life, above and below this table,
tintinnabulates with sweet sweet cantaloupe.

ALI MOHAMED, Hyenas
ELIZABETH GILBERT, Cheekbone

AMIRA AL SAMMRAI, Breathing in the Rain
RICHARD BLANCO, Burning in the Rain

CHRISTINA MURRAY, Carrots
JONATHAN LETHEM, Carrot-Spotting

COLIN SHEPARD, Wildernesses
BILL ROORBACH, Heat Rises

ELIAS NASRAT, The Fate of the Trees
BETSY SHOLL, That Leafless Tree

HASSAN JEYLANI, A Day in Three Worlds
CAMPBELL MCGRATH, Night and Day

JULIAN MAYORQUIN, Bottle Jacking
GEORGE SAUNDERS, Go to Jail, After Eight Times, Go Directly to Jail

RICHARD AKERA, I Started to Explain
RICHARD RUSSO, Drinking Water

VASSILY MURANGIRA, Swimming to Safety
ANN BEATTIE, Drive-by Alligator

JANET MATHIESON, A Sandwich/An Olive
ARI MEIL, Jammy Brightness

MAHAD HILOWLE, The Table
SUSAN CONLEY, The Table

DARCIE SERFES, The Bump
LILY KING, Summer

NOAH WILLIAMS, Hunting in the Deep Woods
LEWIS ROBINSON, When Dad Rode Past Me

MICHÉE RUNYAMBO, Two Teeth
MONICA WOOD, History Lesson

EMILY HOLLYDAY, Cantaloupe
GIBSON FAY-LEBLANC, Self-Portrait, with Dish Rag

## MISSOURI ALICE WILLIAMS, A Little Secret
## MELISSA COLEMAN, Goddess of Liberation

FADUMO ISSACK, Climbing Barefoot
JAED COFFIN, The Coconut Tree

GRACE WHITED, Box of Hope
DAVE EGGERS, Pull the Sled, Feed the Fire

AQILA SHARAFYAR, The Faithful Doves of My Father
SARA CORBETT, I Thought I Could Fix Things

ARUNA KENYI, The Photograph
MICHAEL PATERNITI, We Are Trying to Understand What Happened to You There

# A Little Secret

*Missouri Alice Williams*

There was this girl I knew.
She wasn't very nice.
I met her in high school,
and all I can remember her doing
is slithering that cigarette out of her mouth
and going *pffffffffff*
and blowing a little secret
to the boys.
She had blond curly hair
and then
the next day
she had black curly hair.
But
the thing I remembered the most
is that
whenever she would take her leather jacket off
all you would see
were these huge things
and all the boys would go,
"Yahoo."

# Goddess of Liberation

*Melissa Coleman*

I wish I could be like Tara. She has super thick long black hair, olive skin, round dark eyes, and is starting to get boobs. I have short hair, a million freckles, and a flat chest.

Tara's parents are still married to each other, a honey-blonde mother with a thrilling laugh and tall, math-minded, Spanish-blooded father. My parents are divorced, and I live with my dad and stepmom. Tara and I both landed here this year, at a boarding school in Vermont where our parents teach. We're in seventh grade, and things are about to change—again. We are about to become teenagers.

We're hanging out in my dad's office with a view of round-hilled fields, and we're putting on the Wide Mouth Frog Show. It's Tara's invention because she wants to be an actress so she can move back to California.

"The host always talks in an exaggeratedly slow voice," she explains.

"Welcome to—the Wiiiiddddeee Mouuuuttthh Froooog Shooooow." She swings her arms round to mimic the O of her mouth. "We're so glaaaaad you cooooould joooooooin us."

We don't know it yet, but soon the Wide Mouth Frog Show will go off the air. Tara and I will become boy crazy, and henceforth we'll spend our time writing teen-Harlequin romances in our journals.

Tara will want to do more than just imagine falling in love with a guy, but for me, the imagined version is much less terrifying. "Because look what happened to your mother," the little voice pss, pss, psses in the back of my mind. "Not good. Don't let your guard down. Don't let it happen to you."

"Tooodayyy we have a speeecial gueeeeest," Tara wide mouths. "Mrs. Coooow." She's stealing a little bit of her pronunciation from the Church

Ladies on *Saturday Night Live*, which we've just begun staying up late to watch on sleepovers. I shuffle onto the stage in my white tablecloth and say, "Moo."

I don't remember why I was a cow, but it was probably because we were in Vermont and there were lots of cows around and they were pitifully female, with their ungainly udders and slow eyes.

Back when I was little, before my parents separated and my mother left, I loved being a girl, with my long hair and the free feeling of wearing dresses. I loved that my body was smooth all over without vulnerable and unprotected things hanging loose between my legs or on my chest. Being a girl meant everything was safe inside.

After the divorce, when I lived in Massachusetts with my dad and stepmom, I thought being a boy would solve my problems. My favorite book was *Harriet the Spy*, about a girl who dresses like a boy and writes things about people in her notebook. Later, someone told me Harriet was probably gay and liked girls. I didn't like girls in that way, I just didn't want to be one, and so I lost the power of what I'd learned from Harriet—the importance of loving yourself no matter what you are.

What was I? All I knew is I wanted to stay neutral. Safe. Like Switzerland. Psychiatrists could say these are symptoms of sexual abuse, but I have no memory of that, just a vague post-divorce fear of the world beyond my borders.

"Tell me abooooout your life," Tara says. "Do you like being a coooow?"

"It's not so great," I might say. "I have to have babies and get milked all the time. I'm fat and have big udders that make it hard to walk."

Becoming a woman, from what I'd seen, was not worth the trouble. My mother fell in love and had babies and big boobs and then my sister died and my father left her and she lives alone now. Things are hard for her. Work your fingers to the bone, she says. I know now she was a good wife and mother underneath the pain, and my father was a good father and husband; he simply didn't love my mother in the way she needed to love herself.

Tara's mother seems to enjoy being female, she's easy in her body and around people and her husband. She doesn't work; her job is her kids, she says. She always seems to enjoy her life. Tara and her mother are showing me it can feel good to be beautiful and feminine. It can even be fun!

"A biiiig cheer for Mrs. Cooooow," Tara croons. "Noooow, oooon to our next guest!"

Sometimes Tara worried about being overweight and wished she was tall and slim like her sister, but she always seemed to love herself and her body nonetheless—even through her own parents' divorce, her father's death. This, I know now, was her secret.

In high school and college, boys will be chasing after Tara while I'll be "accidentally" locking my bike to the bikes of boys I like so they will notice me. In our twenties, she'll be standing on a green lawn in California in a white lace wedding dress with flawless skin and dark swoop of hair, while I'll be heartbroken over yet another failed relationship.

I'll want to say it's because she's more beautiful, has bigger boobs, a less difficult past. I'll want to believe there's something wrong with me, that I'm not sexy enough, am too spacey and talk too much, have acne-prone skin and big ears—and for these and many more reasons I'm unlovable. And as long as I believe all this, it will be true and there will be reasons for it to be true.

Then the day comes, after lots of digging around in my heart, that I find I don't believe it anymore. I realize all that yucky stuff is just normal, hard, fascinating human stuff. I look into the eyes of a man I love and find the vulnerability of truly being seen is only scary if you aren't okay with what you are.

Every so often Tara and I like to reminisce about the good ole days of the Wide Mouth Frog Show, back when we were just kids pretending to be frogs or cows, or what have you, busy as we are now with the real life shows of our own husbands, kids, careers, and hopes for a meaningful life.

"By the way," Tara says, "many of the things that worried you were very similar to things that were poking little holes in my soul and self-worth. I wonder how different it might be if we could've shed light then on all that we were hiding within ourselves."

Being a grownup isn't so very different from a teenager, except for the perspective. Every day I must push myself from that neutered shell into the frightening and exposed and beautiful and strong place of my unique self. Because only when I honor and share what I am, am I truly safe.

Yahooooo!

ALI MOHAMED, Hyenas
ELIZABETH GILBERT, Cheekbone

AMIRA AL SAMMRAI, Breathing in the Rain
RICHARD BLANCO, Burning in the Rain

CHRISTINA MURRAY, Carrots
JONATHAN LETHEM, Carrot-Spotting

COLIN SHEPARD, Wildernesses
BILL ROORBACH, Heat Rises

ELIAS NASRAT, The Fate of the Trees
BETSY SHOLL, That Leafless Tree

HASSAN JEYLANI, A Day in Three Worlds
CAMPBELL MCGRATH, Night and Day

JULIAN MAYORQUIN, Bottle Jacking
GEORGE SAUNDERS, Go to Jail, After Eight Times, Go Directly to Jail

RICHARD AKERA, I Started to Explain
RICHARD RUSSO, Drinking Water

VASSILY MURANGIRA, Swimming to Safety
ANN BEATTIE, Drive-by Alligator

JANET MATHIESON, A Sandwich/An Olive
ARI MEIL, Jammy Brightness

MAHAD HILOWLE, The Table
SUSAN CONLEY, The Table

DARCIE SERFES, The Bump
LILY KING, Summer

NOAH WILLIAMS, Hunting in the Deep Woods
LEWIS ROBINSON, When Dad Rode Past Me

MICHÉE RUNYAMBO, Two Teeth
MONICA WOOD, History Lesson

EMILY HOLLYDAY, Cantaloupe
GIBSON FAY-LEBLANC, Self-Portrait, with Dish Rag

MISSOURI ALICE WILLIAMS, A Little Secret
MELISSA COLEMAN, Goddess of Liberation

**FADUMO ISSACK, Climbing Barefoot**
**JAED COFFIN, The Coconut Tree**

GRACE WHITED, Box of Hope
DAVE EGGERS, Pull the Sled, Feed the Fire

AQILA SHARAFYAR, The Faithful Doves of My Father
SARA CORBETT, I Thought I Could Fix Things

ARUNA KENYI, The Photograph
MICHAEL PATERNITI, We Are Trying to Understand What Happened to You There

# Climbing Barefoot

*Fadumo Issack*

When a child is born she learns how to walk, how to eat, how to talk, and how to play. When I was growing up I learned all of these things too; but for me, there was something else just as important—I learned how to climb trees. They became a part of my body; the tree limbs, my limbs. I climbed trees every day.

When I climbed up a tree's branches I felt safe. I climbed as high as I could, and then I would sit down and look out over the only place I had ever known: Ifo, Dadaab, Kenya. Dadaab is the largest refugee camp in the world, and Ifo is where I lived in the middle of it. Trees are rare there, as there are too many people in one area, and men and boys walk many miles to find firewood, leaving women and girls home to face what may come. But there were a few trees near me, which I climbed every day, and one that was the tallest of all, which I would only climb once.

Never for a second did I blame the tree for what happened to me. I never thought, "Maybe if I hadn't been in the tree, my life wouldn't be like this." My relatives thought this way. But for me, it wasn't the tree's fault. It wasn't Ifo's fault, either. I knew Ifo like a book you memorized, and when I looked down from the top of the tree, the camp looked like a good place. I saw kids playing. When I climbed back down, it was a mess, but up there, I felt like everything was okay. I never thought that something bad could happen up there. But it did.

It was a very hot afternoon, the first time I climbed the tree. It hadn't rained for three or four months. I had been walking to the markets to get sugar. I was five years old. When I went back outside, my neighbor called me over to his house. He was twelve. I had known him my whole life. His brothers and sisters and some of the other kids from A-7 block were in his yard. His parents sat in the shadows of their house. My neighbor dared me to climb the acacia tree in the yard, the tallest tree in Ifo. I had never climbed it before. I wasn't scared, though.

I walked up to the tree, took off my sandals, and began to climb. Even though my mom told me always to wear sandals, I liked climbing barefoot. It felt good to feel the tree on my feet and toes. I got to the top very quickly. It was easy for me. I sat down on the highest branch and looked at everybody. None of the kids could believe it. The boy who had dared me to climb the tree said that he didn't think I was really a girl, because I didn't seem to be afraid of anything. Right after he said that he began to climb up the tree, too.

At first I didn't even notice. I was yelling down to another kid. He climbed up and sat on the branch next to where I was sitting. He wanted me to be afraid of him and his family, because everyone else was. But I wasn't. God made me, and God made him; why should I be afraid of him?

He said to me, "Your mom must be proud of you for being so brave." And then he pushed me out of the tree.

People as far away as A-4 block heard my screams. Later they said that I was a quiet girl and they had never heard me scream like that. My father heard me, too, and he ran to find me, lying on the ground. He carried me home. When I woke up later, he was next to me, splashing water all over me. I tried to get up, but every part of my body—my joints, my bones, my skin—hurt. I couldn't move. I was just lying there like a dead person.

My father began to read the Qur'an over me. He did that for such a long time. I fell asleep and woke up; fell asleep and woke up. I was confused and in so much pain. They took me to the hospital and we met the doctors. They examined me and really tried to help, but because I had broken so many bones and joints they didn't know what to do. They didn't know how to cure me.

It was a painful year for all of us, family and me. We couldn't do anything to bring justice to what had happened. Our neighbors were dangerous, and they had killed a lot of people we knew. Whenever my dad wasn't out looking for some way to help me, he read the Qur'an over me. For months, he had looked for miracles from Allah, for some way or for someone who could help me somehow. Then one day he approached this man, a specialist who burned broken bones to heal the person, an old technique from back home in Somalia. The man came.

I remember I cried so loud when he burned my skin. I screamed my nearest brother's name out, and cried, "Please help me! Take me away!" My brother broke into tears. My mom did, too.

It took many more months to heal the burns. Pain became my friend. It told me when I was seriously injured, it kept me awake and angry, but the best thing about it was that it let me know that I was alive. And each day I began to feel a little better. One day I could lift my hand. Another day I could stand up. Finally, I was able to walk again.

The first day that I was strong enough to stand on my own and walk, I walked out of the bedroom, across my yard, and right to a tree. Even though I hadn't climbed in months, my body remembered how. I put my bare foot on the tree, and reached my arm up to the closest branch, and my brain helped my body move in the way it knew so well. I climbed and moved as though nothing had ever happened to me, even though so much had. When I reached the top of the tree and looked out over Ifo again, my eyes began to tear, but for the first time in so long, I cried with joy.

I realized that so much had changed within me since the last time I had sat high up in the trees. I was now seeing with new eyes—as a stronger and wiser person, very different from others. Looking out over my block, at my house, the place I knew so well, I knew that there would be more hard times in my life to come, but that I would have the strength to meet them. I also knew that there would be many joys in my life. I didn't know it then, but I would one day leave the refugee camp and move to the United States with my family.

I looked down at one of my hands where I had a scar from the burning. I have round scars on both of my hands and my ankles. Sometimes it feels good to wear a scar on the outside to represent something on the inside.

# The Coconut Tree

*Jaed Coffin*

In my mother's village, there was a single coconut tree that rose above our family home like a very tall flagpole. The tree stood maybe thirty feet tall, and the trunk was rough and tan and even looked like the trunks of the working elephants that, when my mother was a child, used to pass through the village on their way to and from the lumber camps. At the top of the coconut tree there were a dozen or so mint-colored, finger-like palm fronds; hidden beneath the fronds were maybe six or seven dried up, brown coconuts. But among the dead brown coconuts there was a single green one.

When I was five, or maybe six, or perhaps eight years old—we went to the village often when I was a boy, and my memories of those trips have blended into a single memory that often plays in my head like a running dream—I became very interested in finding a way to get that green coconut down.

I didn't have a whole lot else going on: I didn't speak much Thai then—I still don't—and there was not much for me to do in the village besides sit on the front steps of our home and sip on bottles of green Fanta and munch packets of dry noodles with MSG powder sprinkled on top. Sometimes I played footbahn with the boys from the village who wandered the narrow alleys of our neighborhood like the packs of feral, sore-faced dogs who slept in the temple grounds at night, but I always felt like those boys didn't really want me around, and would just as soon play their footbahn without me.

Other than my sister and mother, the only person in the village who I really could hang out with was my grandfather. He lived in our family home with my uncle and his wife and their two daughters. My grandmother had died some twenty years before I was born—though her ashes were sealed inside the temple walls, behind a square tile adorned with her photograph—and so my grandfather spent a lot of time sitting next to me on the steps, peeling and cutting fruit while staring off into the distance, sometimes sighing in that very Thai way of sighing which is similar to the American sigh but has a higher pitched, more animal, and I think less complaining ring to it. It is between sighing and crying, really, and so does not sound so pitiful.

My grandfather dressed like all the old men in the village: in cloth shirts with wide necks and buttons and big pockets down the front, in wide-legged cloth pants that tied in the front. He wore single-strap leather sandals whose soles held the deep impressions of his toes and heels. My grandfather also had lots of black hair that he slicked back with some kind of oil. His skin was very dark: whenever I try to remember what it looked like, the image of a heavily oiled teak wood statue of Confucius comes to my mind. That statue still stands in my mother's house.

My mother always told me that my grandfather was a medicine man, a word I don't exactly know how to say in Thai but which I think is something like *maw thammachat*, or "nature doctor." Every morning, I would watch my grandfather load a dozen or so empty glass bottles into the basket hanging off the handlebars of his purple bicycle. Then he would ride off into the forests beyond our village. When he returned later in the day, the bottles would all be full of plants and leaves and root-looking things, which he would then use to make ointments and salves. There was a shelf over the kitchen that was full of those bottles, and they sat next to photographs of our deceased ancestors. There was a picture of a great-grandfather whom my mother had once told me had owned a banana plantation and had eight wives, and she still remembers visiting each of them, one after another, in a long canal boat. There was also a picture of my grandmother on that shelf, and next to her portrait was a Buddha statue and a little pot of incense. Sometimes, when I couldn't sleep at night because of the twelve hours of jetlag between Maine and Thailand, I would sit up and listen to my grandfather chanting Pali sutras in front of the picture, the smell of burning incense drifting through the mosquito net that hung over the bed that I shared with my mother and sister. When I woke up in the mid-morning I would sometimes find him sleeping upon a wooden platform, upon a straw mat, one arm over his eyes, snoring loudly while motorcycles zipped back and forth across the wooden bridge over the canal.

While my grandfather was in the forest collecting plants one day, I decided that I was going to climb the coconut tree. Without telling my mother, I wandered away from our house, wrapped my arms around the trunk, and tried to inch my way up. I got a few feet up, slid down a few feet, climbed a few feet higher. Then, I think I got a little bit scared, so I slid back down.

Part of the problem was that I was wearing sandals—my mother always told me and my sister that we were never to walk around the village barefoot, even though all the other kids in the village did. "The village is very dirty," she often told us. "You will step on glass and get an infection and your foot will rot." A few years earlier we had come to the village and my sister had gotten some kind of yellow fever, and her eyes had crusted shut and I think she might have almost died had my uncle not been a doctor in the king's hospital in Bangkok. So maybe my mother was still trying to reconcile how the very country where she had lived most of her life was also a place that was capable of killing her fragile American children.

I stared up at the single green coconut hanging there, and steeled myself to give it another shot. Just as I wrapped my arms around the trunk, the pack of boys came along, tossing a plastic soccer ball between them, laughing and pointing at me. One of them, a very good looking kid who was the best at footbahn, smiled at me, kicked off his flip flops, and shimmied up the tree like a monkey. With one hand, he ripped down the coconut and then he tossed it down to his friends, who tried to catch it but didn't. The boy picked up the coconut and held it out to me. "You want it? You want it?" he said. "Ao mai?"—as the other boys laughed behind him.

"No," I said. "I don't want it. Mai ao."

The boy smiled at me then tossed the coconut on the ground. Then he and the other boys disappeared down an alley.

I picked up the coconut and tried to open it with a wooden sword that I'd bought at the market, but the skin was too tough and the sword was too dull. Some of the women who sold papaya salad near the temple grounds saw me, and they offered to cut the coconut open with the big machetes they used to chop green papaya, but I pretended I didn't understand them and carried the coconut inside our house.

While I waited for my grandfather to come home from the forest, I couldn't stop thinking about how that kid showed me up. So I went outside barefoot, intending to climb the tree just as he had. As soon as I put my bare feet on the trunk of the tree I felt nimble and powerful and brave again, and I climbed up high enough so that the women at the papaya salad carts took notice of me, and then I slid down. I'm not sure where my mother was—she was in high demand in the village, because, though she was only a nurse, everyone assumed she had tons of money—but I took that moment of rare freedom to walk around the village barefoot for a while.

I was wandering along the canal when I felt a quick slicing sensation on the sole of my foot. When I lifted my foot there was a long bleeding incision between my big and little toes, with little folds of skin and fat curling out from inside the incision. I looked around: at the pregnant dogs with sores on their mouths, the motherless kittens that were sometimes disposed of in overflowing trash cans, at a world that, in that singular moment, seemed to thrum with a humid, fecal danger.

My mother was waiting for me at home. She told me to sit down and then she washed my foot out with water, working quickly, and I could tell that in her mind she was angry and worried and confused all at once. She put a towel on my foot and held it there, firmly, while studying the features of her former home: the metal roof that made lots of noise during rainy season monsoons; the dusty window sills and the dusty table and the mosquito nets and the big ceramic jugs that collected rainwater that was used to flush the pit toilet. All of it was a threat to whatever she was building in her other life, far away. Hers were not so much questions of loyalty as careful calculations of degrees of sacrifice.

And then my grandfather came back from the forest, the bottles of plants and roots and leaves rattling in the basket. "Unh! Bah!" he said, and waved my mother aside, and then he lifted my foot and removed the towel and studied the incision. He looked at me and then at the incision again and then he reached onto the shelf and took down a bottle of ointment: This one had a long root in it, and the liquid in the bottle was brown-green and swampy, and in the opening of the bottle was a cork.

He dabbed at the cut with a swab of ointment, opened the cut wider, dabbed some more, and then kept dabbing, and dabbing, and dabbing, and dabbing, and now for some reason my memory of that afternoon stops there—the dabbing—and it does not resume until a time that must have occurred some several days later. What I recall then was how the cut had healed, entirely, without any scar or scab. I have no idea what my grandfather did to my foot, I have no idea what plant was used in that ointment; no one in the village possesses that kind of knowledge anymore, and I don't think people even in rural Thailand have much interest in reviving that kind of knowledge now that there are faster ways to do things. I don't even know if what I remember about how quickly the cut healed is in fact true. I really don't know.

But I suppose when you have a memory like that—of an old man who, soon after, would be cremated in the temple grounds and disappear into the hazy sky in a column of dark smoke, his ashes buried, too, in the walls of the temple in a small cubby facing his wife—it has to mean something. It has to be symbolic of something you needed to understand at the time. Right? Right? It doesn't just kick around your head for no reason. Right?

I think of all the incisions in my mother's life at that time—cultural, romantic, familial, linguistic—and I have to wonder if perhaps the reason I remember that story so vividly is because I needed to make sense of our life in a way that, as a boy, I just couldn't.

And then, a few days later now, the memory starts moving again: I'm sitting with my grandfather, the coconut chopped open with a rusty machete, him showing me how to sit on this wooden stool-like contraption with a blade on one end that I think was called a "rabbit" because it looked like one, and in the old days was used to remove coconut meat from its shell.

"Bah! Bah!" my grandfather says, as he rakes the inside of the coconut over the blade, the filets of the white meat sliding loose into a silver platter, then him handing me the coconut—"Bah! Bah! Take it!"—to try it myself, and then him offering me the meat, too, and telling me to "Gin! Gin! Gin!" which is Thai for "Eat! Eat! Eat!"

# Box of Hope

*Grace Whited*

In a tiny village on the western shores of Japan, an origami box is born in the knobby hands of an old Japanese man with a long, white beard and wrinkles beneath his eyes. He folds the box tenderly beneath the glow of a candle's light.

The origami box is neon green on the outside with a checkered pink and navy blue pattern inside. Four triangular flaps peek out from the inside, all pointing in the cardinal directions like wings ready to fly. The bottom of the box is flat and about one inch deep, as it must protect its light wherever it may go.

In the deep of the night, the old man carries the box away from his workshop toward the edge of the ocean. Waves lap gently onto the soft sand as he kneels down onto the shore. The old man's wife, a petite but strong woman, appears behind him, a lit candle cupped in her hands. Gradually, more people appear onto the beach, one by one.

Once a year, the people of the village come to the shore bearing origami boxes to honor the loved ones they have lost. The candle that is placed in the center of the box represents each bygone soul. The elderly couple comes to honor the daughter they lost fifty years ago from a sickness that took her life when she was only seven.

The old man's wife kneels down beside him, placing the candle inside the box. Along the shoreline, others do the same. Then the villagers release their own tiny boxes into the ocean, candlelight glowing at their centers.

Together they stand, linking hands and watching the flicker of the candlelight float away with the tide. Eventually, when the boxes carry the light of the candles out of sight, the people of the village disperse without a word. Along with their origami boxes, the villagers have released the sadness and regret that came from their losses, and replaced them with hope.

The old man's box is carried away from the seas of Japan and lands on the soft, white sands of a distant shore where a young girl with shattered dreams for the future finds it. Her parents have recently divorced, and she blames herself for their separation.

The girl wonders every day if she could have done something to keep them together. Her father, noticing she has seemed distraught lately, has taken her on a vacation. The young girl is walking along the beach when a flash of neon green in a tangle of seaweed catches her eye. Kneeling down, the girl scoops up the box ever so gently.

The candle has long since burnt out and the paper has been damaged by the elements, but she still thinks it is the most beautiful thing she has ever seen. Balancing the tiny box in her hands, the little girl is amazed that it has come so far. The origami box is so tiny, so fragile, yet it has still has found its way to her. The little girl believes that if the box could survive its journey, although battered and a little damaged, she can survive the hardships she is going through. Standing up, the box nestled in her hands, the young girl faces the rising sun with a new sense of bravery in her heart.

Spinning around, the little girl runs back to the beach house she and her father are staying in. Throwing open the front door, the origami box still clutched in her hand, the little girl confronts her father. After the girl tearfully admits she blames herself for the separation, her father assures her it was not her fault, and the little girl could have done nothing to help it.

It takes a few months and an abundance of reassurance from her parents until the girl comes to accept the fact that she could do nothing to keep her parents together. Although the little girl no longer feels the need for the box anymore, she keeps it by her side everywhere she goes. Eventually, she grows up and falls in love. She and her beloved are happily wedded, and after a few years she has a son.

The little boy is crippled, paralyzed from the waist down. His heart is frail and does not work properly. He spends his days in a clean, white hospital room, his wheelchair by the window, an IV in his arm. The little boy watches happy children walk down the street outside his window. He curses his crippled legs, scratching them until they bleed.

The time comes for hope, and his mother hands him the origami box. The little boy is overjoyed. Since he has no friends who will visit him and he is incapable of leaving the hospital, this tiny box is the most important connection the little boy has to the outside world.

The box is now old and worn, its once bright colors are faded, but his mother has taken good care of it since she was a child. The box resembles its creator, the old Japanese man, and is a little tattered around the edges but still standing strong. Cradling it gently in his hands, the little boy vows never to let it go as he thanks his mother over and over again.

Eventually, the little boy goes through surgery, his weak heart is fixed, and he is permitted to leave the hospital for the first time in his life. As the little boy is wheeled through the doors, he holds the box in his lap. When he goes to school for the first time, the children stare. There are hushed voices as he wheels himself down the hallways, and he almost wishes for the solitary comfort of his hospital room.

When the teacher asks a question, he thinks of the box at home, and his hand is the first one up. Whispered conversations are exchanged behind his back. "Have you seen the new boy?" They make him wilt inside but, again, he thinks of the box sitting on top of his dresser, holds his head high, ignoring the hushed gossip.

The first glimmer of hope appears during lunch, when a girl in the same grade as the little boy slides into the seat across from him. She is of Asian descent with dark eyes warm with good intention. When she introduces herself, the little boy smiles for the first time that day. The girl is the only student who has spoken to him at all yet.

The two become good friends, and eventually the little boy shows the little girl his special origami box. She comments on how old and worn it's gotten and asks the little boy if he would like for her to teach him how to make another one. The little boy nods eagerly.

By the end of the afternoon, a new origami box perches in the little boy's hands. The inside is pastel pink and light tangerine, while the outside is bright pink, like the skin of an infant taking a breath for the very first time.

# Pull the Sled,
# Feed the Fire

*Dave Eggers*

In this glorious winter landscape of gentle white hills and cream-dolloped pines and air so pure it cleanses every capillary, the man is cursing his wife and his wife's mother. It was his mother-in-law who said this hike would be easy, that this hike was only a mile or so, and it was his wife who tacitly endorsed this theory. But the hike feels like much more than a mile, in part because they—the mother-in-law is not on this hike; she is at home and warm—are trudging up a steep hill, a drastic hill, and also because it is December, and because there is five feet of snow on the ground, and they are wearing snowshoes. Also the man is carrying a forty-pound pack on his back while strapped into a harness, like a mule, pulling a sled carrying his two small children. Together the children weigh seventy pounds, and the sled is ten pounds, and the pack is forty pounds, so he is pulling 130 or so pounds uphill while wearing snowshoes, and his heart is pounding in an unfamiliar way, a way that implies it will burst and he will die here, on this hill, in front of his family, on the way to a yurt.

Why are they hiking to this yurt in the middle of December? Because the mother-in-law, who is from a farm in Sweden and whom he loves and respects without limit, said this hike would be not only beautiful but a cinch, "so easy," she said, in her accent, which is lovable and extreme. Everything is easy for her, because she grew up on this farm, roping cows and slaughtering things and cross-country skiing to school every day, passing wild boars and ice-fishermen and farmhouses where Jewish girls were hiding from the Nazis.

So the man is cursing her and her strength and her cavalier attitude toward endeavors like this, endeavors that might kill him. He feels half-certain that he will die here, pulling a sled, with his small children watching him collapse in the snow, grabbing his bursting heart. They will have no options to save him, of course, being twenty miles from the closest hospital. They will have to bury him here.

He rests. He looks back at his children, who are eating snow, and looks at his wife, who is adjusting her snowshoes, which are old and broken. Her mother said the snowshoes were fine, but they are not fine, and now, thank God, his wife is complaining about her mother, too. So he rests, waiting for his heart to slow down, breathing in the cold air, looking around at the Idaho landscape, which is magnificent. They are in hill country, the slopes dotted with thirty-foot pines, with the occasional rock outcropping, the land unpopulated as far as you can see, everything white, the snow heavy and arranged in rococo curves, like cream dumped, with bold flourishes, from a spoon.

It begins to snow. The man turns up toward the path and begins again. He finds that he can take about twenty steps before needing to rest again, his heart slapping around his sternum like a fish in a bucket, and while he rests he says nothing, because if he allows himself to talk he will curse his mother-in-law, and he doesn't want to do that, for she produced his wife, whom he loves, always and endlessly, but much more so since she began cursing his mother-in-law, too, out loud.

He begins upward again and soon the path turns toward a forest of pine. He has been given a map to the yurt, but the map is incomplete, and ahead there is a fork in the path, and the map does not tell him where to go. He curses the mapmaker. If he has to drag this 100-pound load farther than necessary, or worse, double back to do any of this trail twice, he will find the mapmaker and kill the mapmaker.

They continue on. The path gets rougher and the children fall out of the sled. The man removes the harness from his chest and goes to pick up the children and put them back on the sled. They are now red-faced and wet, and he knows he will have to get to the yurt faster, before they freeze, for they are tiny and helpless.

The snow begins to fall more heavily. He takes another thirty steps and rests. He wipes the snow from his face. Another thirty steps and they are in the pine forest. The route is more difficult to discern in the forest; around every tree the path seems to disappear. The man has to guess at the path, a terrible course of action while the children shiver and his heart continues to try to escape from his ribcage. Finally, they see a yurt, and there is a brief rejoicing by all, but this is not the correct yurt. They keep going. The man is soaked in sweat, though the air outside is twenty degrees Fahrenheit. They pass a few more yurts, none of which are theirs. Occasionally they see the tracks of a snowmobile and the man curses himself for not asking the owners of the yurt for a ride on the snowmobile. When they were being outfitted, and the outfitters were showing him how to harness himself, like a mule, to the sled, the snowmobile ride had been offered, but the man had agreed with his mother-in-law that he could do it, that it was not too far.

But now it seems too far, and the sun is setting. The man knows that if it gets dark before they get close, they will not find the yurt. There will be no chance. Do they have a flashlight? He can't remember. It's getting dark, quickly, and the trees are getting denser. In seconds any sign of the sun is gone and the only light remaining is vestigial and weak. The snow goes from orange to blue to grey as they trudge on, the land flat now. They know they can't rest until they arrive.

The forest gets darker, the shapes vaguer. What seems to be a yurt just ahead to the east, is only a downed tree. The path is no longer visible, for the fallen snow has erased it. They can only try to stay straight, given the map, drawn by a madman, says the yurt is straight ahead. The children are now worried about the darkness, which is nearing absolute, and the man is worried about the darkness, too, but he says they are close. He says he is sure about it. He is not sure, but almost as soon as the lie escapes his mouth, he sees it.

There it is, a yurt. They see the number on the yurt and it corresponds with the number they rented. They have no time to celebrate. The kids' feet are wet and cold and they need to build a fire. Inside the yurt there is an old pot-bellied stove and a stack of wood. The man gets to work on the fire while the woman and the kids take off their wet clothes. The parents touch their children's feet, and they try not to make terrified sounds. Their feet are frozen. There needs to be a fire in this stove very soon or both children, especially the tiny boy, just three years old, will be in bad shape.

The fire starts. But the heat is not penetrating the yurt. The fire does not seem to be warming anything but the iron that contains it. So they gather around the fire. The man puts the children's feet close to the stove and he and their mother take the little feet in their hands and massage them. Such tiny toes, much too cold.

Soon the fire is roaring, and the heat is warming the yurt. The little feet are getting back to a human temperature, warm enough to ensconce in dry wool socks. The feet safe, the children not dying, the family begins to unpack and look around the yurt. There are two futons, now in the shape of couches. There is a bookshelf with some games—Old Maid, Battleship, Chutes and Ladders.

The kids play the games while they are eating crackers they've brought. Their mother is boiling snow to have something to drink. She fills a pitcher-sized pot with snow and finds that it yields a few tablespoons of water.

With everyone occupied and the fire going, the man now has to go outside and close the flaps on the windows. The yurt has three large plastic windows, and each plastic window has a flap of heavy vinyl that needs to be unrolled, to further warm the interior. The man, who is lazy and never learns anything, does not put on his snowshoes before going outside, and immediately he regrets it, as his feet sink four feet into the snow. But it's too late to put the snowshoes on now; there is no point. So he walks around the yurt, unraveling each window-flap as quickly as possible. By the time he does so, his feet are soaked and cold, and he has to start over inside, this time warming his own feet.

The man puts his wet socks on the stove's exterior to dry them, and finds that it works quickly. He puts the kids' socks there, too, and they are soon dry. His son's coat is wet, too, so he puts that on the stove. Feeling like everything is in order, and the yurt is warm, the man sits down to play a game with the kids. They play, feeling content that they have created a suitable environment for themselves.

But now his son is coughing. And his daughter is coughing. And his wife's eyes are watering. His own throat is burning. What is happening? The man checks the fire, which seems to be fine. Is the flue broken? The yurt is filled with smoke. His wife rushes to the door and opens it. But this has little effect; the air is thick with acrid smoke, and the two parents are frantic. They bring their children to the yurt door and shove their heads into the fresh air. Soon they're all standing outside the yurt, where it's dark and no more than fifteen degrees Fahrenheit. The man goes back inside to see if he can determine why the stove, which was working fine before, is now billowing smoke into the yurt.

He sees the coat. It's on top of the stove, green smoke curling extravagantly from it. He grabs it and sees that because the coat is made of plastic, half of it has melted onto the stove. The fumes in the tent are toxic. He takes the coat and throws it outside, where his family is, and he knows that all this was his fault. Why didn't he know that a plastic coat should not be put on a hot stove?

Then again, who would make a coat out of plastic? They go outside, the children's coughing sending the mother and father into paroxysms of guilt, the two of them exchanging looks of quiet panic. Periodically, they check in the yurt to see if the fumes are less deadly. Ten minutes pass, then twenty, as they keep their limbs moving outside, in the dark. They hear the distant warnings of an owl. Above, snow drifts lazily down through the dense interlocking branches above.

Finally it's livable within again, and they go inside, though they keep the door open and stay near it. As they gulp clean air from the Idaho night, and hope they will be able to sleep inside what was very recently a toxic oven, no one, not even his wife, tells the man he is a fool. There is no need to tell him he is a fool, because this is self-evident and beyond debate: He was a few minutes from asphyxiating his family.

Eventually the air inside is clean. The man and the woman take deep breaths to make sure they taste nothing chemical. Satisfied, they close the front door. They cook and the kids eat quickly and thoroughly.

The parents unfold the futons and push them together, arranging the mattresses, as thick and sturdy as bread, into one large bed. They find and read from a children's chapter book of incomprehensible folk tales, and when they're done, the fire has died down, and the man has to feed it again with kindling and logs. The stove is eating wood far quicker than he thought possible, and he finds himself feeding it every fifteen minutes. He wonders how this will work, then, while they're all sleeping—how will they maintain adequate heat?

The answer comes soon. After the kids are asleep, and their mother is trying to sleep, the man finds himself sitting on the edge of the bed, near the fire, feeding it again. They have arranged the children on the other side of the bed, far from the fire, given the little ones are prone to moving far and erratically while sleeping, and they don't want them turning into the stove and grilling themselves. But because the children are so far from the fire, the man worries about keeping them warm. Every foot away from the fire, the temperature drops ten degrees.

And to keep the fire going, the man needs to keep feeding it. He has just read about Pakistani children, refugees from a conflict he can't name, freezing in the cold at night, dying in their sleep. The man has the feeling that this could happen here, too. What if he falls asleep, close to the fire, and the fire dies, and his children, closer to the door . . .

So, he decides to stay awake. It's ten o'clock now, and there will be eight hours till first light. Not so long to wait. They have nothing in particular to do the next day, so he can sleep then.

He feeds the fire and listens to the world. There is the hungry hiss of the fire, the shushing of his children moving in their sleep. The wind picks up and there is a thump outside. It could be an animal, or a fallen branch, but the man realizes it's snow on the roof that the wind has dislodged and sent to the ground. The thumps continue through the night, as the wind weaves through the trees, alive and predatory.

The time passes slowly. The boy moves his foot from under the covers and the man reaches over to tuck his foot in again. The girl takes her arms out from under the covers and the man puts them under. The man looks so long at the contents of the yurt that he knows everything by heart—the rough-hewn kitchen counter, the kerosene lamp, the old romance novels, the local newspapers, the faces of his wife and children, orange then pink then orange, all of them dreaming peacefully, all of them assuming the fire will continue.

The work of keeping it strong is simple and feels good. The best work is work you know is necessary, is within your ability, and will end. Feeding the fire is that kind of work. The man knows, or believes, he needs to feed the fire all night or else his children will freeze, and he knows the work will end when the sun comes up. He can do it and will do it.

But occasionally he falls asleep. When he wakes up a second time he makes a plan he thinks is smart: He feeds the fire, then he takes off his shirt and lies down, exposing his back to the fire. His idea is that the moment the fire begins to die, his exposed flesh will feel this temperature change immediately, and he will wake up. If he were covered with blankets he might not realize the temperature drop until too late.

It is a ludicrous plan, but it works. His unclothed back feels any drop in temperature quickly, and every time, he wakes up and he feeds the fire again, and then sleeps for another half hour.

And in this way he passes the night. At least until he wakes up at three A.M., when there is a loud pop within the stove as the logs rearrange themselves. He cannot fall back asleep, and decides he doesn't care. He sees that everyone is asleep, with various limbs exposed, which the man quickly covers up. He goes back to the stove, opens the door, and looks inside. He watches the fire for a while, and remembers a classmate of his from high school and college who once confided to him that he knew of a species of creature, much like man but the size of insects, which lived within the flames of fires like this. Only he could see them, he said, but they were very real, and very content there, living amid the embers. The man wonders what became of this classmate-prophet, and then lies on his back, staring at the ceiling of the yurt, listening to the snow shift tectonically above.

By daylight he has slept perhaps three hours, in twenty-minute segments, and he feels tired but exhilarated. His family wakes up and begins to organize the yurt, and as they're cleaning and getting dressed and boiling water, he sees a notice in the yurt that asks all visitors to replenish the woodpile, replacing the pile with the same amount of split wood used during the guests' stay. So he goes outside, removes the tarp from the woodpile and finds an axe, a wedge, and a round. He sets the first log on the round and lifts the axe. When it comes down, it cuts so quickly and easily through the wood that he can only think of diving into water from a high board. It's briefly jarring, when your head hits the water or when the axe strikes the flesh of the wood, but the movement thereafter is so fluid and fast that it feels like life itself. So the man continues to chop the logs into quarters, thinking the axe the most fantastic tool he's ever used, until he's chopped enough wood to replace all that he burned in the interest of keeping his children alive.

The sun has risen now, and is beaming white light through the trees and ice, and the man is soaked in sweat again and happy. He goes inside and drinks terrible coffee, and he and his family talk about how close they were to suffocating in this yurt, and how stupid he is.

They put their snowshoes on again, and load the children onto the sled. The man's wife looks luminous in her heavy wool hat, and his children look so goofy and unknowing, and the man pretends that he was part of some secret adventure in the night, some crucial mission that required his particular skills and perseverance. They lock the yurt and he harnesses himself in, and because the morning is dry and warming, the sun brilliant and sky blue and the path downhill, the man is sure he has never lived a better day.

ALI MOHAMED, Hyenas
ELIZABETH GILBERT, Cheekbone

AMIRA AL SAMMRAI, Breathing in the Rain
RICHARD BLANCO, Burning in the Rain

CHRISTINA MURRAY, Carrots
JONATHAN LETHEM, Carrot-Spotting

COLIN SHEPARD, Wildernesses
BILL ROORBACH, Heat Rises

ELIAS NASRAT, The Fate of the Trees
BETSY SHOLL, That Leafless Tree

HASSAN JEYLANI, A Day in Three Worlds
CAMPBELL MCGRATH, Night and Day

JULIAN MAYORQUIN, Bottle Jacking
GEORGE SAUNDERS, Go to Jail, After Eight Times, Go Directly to Jail

RICHARD AKERA, I Started to Explain
RICHARD RUSSO, Drinking Water

VASSILY MURANGIRA, Swimming to Safety
ANN BEATTIE, Drive-by Alligator

JANET MATHIESON, A Sandwich/An Olive
ARI MEIL, Jammy Brightness

MAHAD HILOWLE, The Table
SUSAN CONLEY, The Table

DARCIE SERFES, The Bump
LILY KING, Summer

NOAH WILLIAMS, Hunting in the Deep Woods
LEWIS ROBINSON, When Dad Rode Past Me

MICHÉE RUNYAMBO, Two Teeth
MONICA WOOD, History Lesson

EMILY HOLLYDAY, Cantaloupe
GIBSON FAY-LEBLANC, Self-Portrait, with Dish Rag

MISSOURI ALICE WILLIAMS, A Little Secret
MELISSA COLEMAN, Goddess of Liberation

FADUMO ISSACK, Climbing Barefoot
JAED COFFIN, The Coconut Tree

GRACE WHITED, Box of Hope
DAVE EGGERS, Pull the Sled, Feed the Fire

**AQILA SHARAFYAR, The Faithful Doves of My Father**
**SARA CORBETT, I Thought I Could Fix Things**

ARUNA KENYI, The Photograph
MICHAEL PATERNITI, We Are Trying to Understand What Happened to You There

# The Faithful Doves of My Father

*Aqila Sharafyar*

My father kept birds—about fifteen beautiful white doves—behind our house in Kabul. He had them as long as I could remember, from the time I was a very small child. My dad loved the birds more than anyone else in my family. He was the one who fed them and cleaned out their cage, which was behind our house and the size of a small room. He went out and talked to them, making little dove calls as he encouraged them to eat. He also put small bangles around their ankles. That way we could hear the birds cooing and jingling while we ate our dinner or sat and talked as a family in the evenings.

I was very young at the time, maybe six or seven years old, and I loved helping my dad with the birds. I loved the way the cage smelled. I liked going in and helping to sprinkle seeds for them on the floor, or bringing them pieces of bread from the house. My older sisters never went into the birdhouse. But I was always with my dad. If he were going to a friend's house, I was with him. Some days I even rode the bus to his work, where he was a manager at a human resources firm. On Fridays, my father went to the mosque to pray. Sometimes, he'd take me with him. I never prayed. I just walked around, playing with the water outside or looking at my reflection in the mirrors hung everywhere.

When the war started in 1992, our lives changed. My dad stopped going to the mosque because it was too dangerous to go there. He stopped going to work every day. At first he went every other day, but after a while he could not travel on the roads. He was scared he'd be killed. Even when we were in our house, bombs exploded overhead, and planes we could see from our window were dropping more of them. Governments in the north and south of our city were shooting each other. The Sunni mostly spoke Pashtun and the Shiaa mostly spoke Farsi, so they not only were fighting about different languages and different religions, but more than anything they were fighting over which group would rule the country.

My family is Shiaa, but my school was mixed—Sunni and Shiia kids grew up together. If the teachers were Sunni, they treated the Sunni kids better than they did the others. In Afghanistan, there are more Sunni than Shiaa people, and they always had the higher power. My older sisters didn't go to school because they were treated poorly there for being Shiaa, for being a lower class. But I loved school, even though the teachers sometimes hit us with sticks or rulers. Even today, if one of my teachers in the U.S. gets mad, I start shaking and I forget everything.

After the war started, I, too, mostly stopped going to school. Our street got really empty. Every house, every family, wanted to move, and a lot of people did move away. They went to Pakistan or to Iran. We stayed in school for a couple of months, but when the war got really bad, my mom wouldn't let us go anymore. I spent my days playing behind our house close to the doves when it was safe to be outside.

Sometimes, though, it wasn't safe at all. It was so dangerous to go out on the streets that we would not get any food. We'd send the men out to climb up into the trees and pick apples for us to eat. When the bombing was that bad, all the neighbors came to my house because we had a basement, and you could hide down there. As the war got worse, everybody came to hide with us. They stayed once for two or three weeks under the ground. Everyone was looking for a safer place to live, trying to decide where to go. We sat together in our basement, eating apples and drinking water, and wondering what to do next.

Even during this time, though, my dad went outside to feed his doves. I remember he used to fuss over their feathers. He sometimes used colorful paint—pinks and greens—and would put little marks on the heads of his favorite birds, just to make them look prettier. And that jingling sound they made because of the bangles he put on their ankles—he loved to hear that, especially when they were all walking at the same time. I remember it sounded a little like raindrops.

The war continued to get worse, though, and my parents thought we should move closer to the city, where it might be safer for us. My dad did not want to leave the birds, but he also knew that he couldn't bring them with us. We were moving into his sister's house and there was no room for them there. So my dad sold the doves to a man who lived in a different neighborhood. We didn't sell our house. We just locked the doors and left.

In downtown Kabul, things weren't much safer. There were fewer explosions than there had been at the old house, but the Sunni mujahideen were gathering on the outskirts of the city and it was becoming more dangerous to be downtown. One day my dad traveled back to our old house to pick up some of our belongings. When he got there, he found all of his doves sitting in our yard and on top of the house, as if they'd been waiting for him. The man who had bought them had left a note on the door for my dad. He wanted his money back because the doves would not stay with him.

We had been living with my aunt for maybe two months by then. The war was just as bad in her neighborhood as it had been in our old neighborhood. My parents were talking about trying to get us to Pakistan, to get out of the country as refugees, but my mom didn't want to. She and my sisters missed the house. My mom said, "We don't want to go to a different country because we don't have enough money. If we go to Pakistan, we're not going to have food to eat or a house to live in, and we're going to die there, too. We've got to go back to our old house."

We did go home again, but something scary happened along the way. We had found a taxi to take us from my aunt's house to our old house, but once we reached our neighborhood, there was a checkpoint. The guards there pulled my dad out of the car and pointed a gun at him, saying that he was Pashtun. They didn't like Pashtun people and were killing them. My dad said, "No, I'm not Pashtun!" But they didn't believe him. My mom screamed and then began crying. We were all crying. Eventually, they let him go and we made it back to the house.

My dad paid the guy who'd bought the doves so they belonged to him again. At this point most of our neighbors had gone. The streets were empty. There were just a few kids left. I used to be able to hear them playing marbles and shouting playfully outside, but now it was so quiet. All the doors were locked. Besides us, only one family of three people was left on the street, good friends of ours. They'd felt afraid living alone, and soon they moved into the lower floor of our house. We were so happy to be back home, to be back with the doves. We had our lives back.

\* \* \*

The day came when everything changed again. I remember it was sunny. The morning began quietly. It felt like there was no war going on in the country. Around ten o'clock, I saw my dad through the window. He was outside, feeding the doves. He looked really calm and different that day, I don't know why.

A couple hours later, I was downstairs with our neighbor, pounding stale bread into pieces to feed to the doves. My mom had gone out to bake bread at a collective bakery. My older sister Yelda was cooking eggplant in the kitchen.

My dad was going out to do errands with my younger sister Maryam, who was three years old then. I was about eight myself. I heard Yelda ask my dad if he could go to the store to get some fresher eggplants. I heard her say good-bye. I wanted to go with them, so I ran outside to try to catch them. But he was gone already, down the street. I followed him for a minute, calling his name. When he heard me, he turned around.

"*Father*, I want to go with you!" I said.

He said, "No. I can't take you. I can't take two kids. It's too dangerous." Then he told me to go home.

"Okay," I said. "But will you bring me some gum?"

I watched him walk down our narrow street, carrying my sister in his arms. Then I went back home.

When he left it was quiet, but soon the bombs started exploding again. It would be quiet for ten minutes, and then more bombs. Some were close. Some were far away. I remember my neighbor yelling for us to get in the basement, where we would be safer. We went down there, I followed Yelda and her eggplants, and a bomb exploded very close by. Yelda was so startled that she dropped her paring knife. We were all shaking. A few minutes later, we heard a group of men's voices coming down our street.

They burst into our house. One of them was carrying my baby sister Maryam, who was bleeding from her head. She was full of shot. They started washing her to see how badly she'd been wounded. She was so quiet that I knew it was serious. The women were all crying. I didn't even think about where my dad was.

One of the guys asked me to take him to find my mother at the bakery. When she saw me walk in, she knew something was wrong. He told my mother to go home quickly. My mom started screaming and crying, dropping her things right onto the floor. When she got home, she found out that my sister had lived, but my dad had been killed. When she heard this, the day became night for her. She has never been the same again.

\* \* \*

We were home when a group of men from the neighborhood opened the gate to our yard and carried my dad's body in on a stretcher. I was upstairs in the house, watching through the window. They laid him down inside the courtyard, close to the doves' house. He was covered with a white cloth.

My mother called for me to come down and say good-bye, but at first I couldn't go. I had no strength in my legs. I felt like I couldn't move. Finally, I made it downstairs to see him. My mom lifted the cloth and put her hand up to close his eyes. We all hugged him and cried.

Even the doves seemed to be crying, making sad sounds, banging their bodies against the wire of the cage as if they wanted to get out. The road to the graveyard had been covered with landmines, so it was too dangerous to take him there. We decided it would be best to bury him next to the house in a small garden belonging to our family.

On the day he was to be buried, he was laid on a stretcher in our backyard. My mom said, "I want the birds to say good bye to him." She opened the cage and let them out. She was talking to him. She said, "These are your birds. I can't take care of them." She was angry—not at him, but at the war. Maryam was still in the hospital. She would be brain-damaged for life. My mom said to my dad's body, "These birds remind me of you. I'm going to let them go away, like you have gone away."

As she opened the door, the doves flew out and, one by one, landed around the stretcher where my dad's body lay. They did not fly away. Some sat in the trees, watching. But they stayed close, sitting all around him. A mullah read from the Qu'ran, and the men lifted the body to carry it to the garden. As they moved, the doves started to follow. They flew behind the men as they walked to the burial site—a long trail of doves following my father to his grave.

\* \* \*

I was fourteen years old when I moved to the United States with my mother and two of my sisters. My two older sisters are married. One lives in Kabul and the other in Canada. Life in Afghanistan was very hard for my mother once she became responsible for taking care of our family by herself. When the Taliban came to power, we lost all our freedoms. Women were not allowed to work anymore, and girls were not allowed to go to school. We were forced to go the mosque seven times a day to pray. If the Taliban caught people on the streets during prayer time, they were arrested and taken away.

I am now a junior at Deering High School in Portland, Maine. My favorite class is English, because I learned it quickly. My two younger sisters go to school here, too, and my mother is learning English at Adult Education. I am thankful for my mom. If it were not for her, I would not live in the United States. I wouldn't have the opportunities for success that I have here. If I had stayed in my country, I would have been married at the age of fourteen—the age I was when I left home. I'd probably have kids, and I wouldn't have a good life.

In my free time, I work at McDonald's because I am saving money to buy a car and go to college. My life has changed a lot here. I am getting an education. I have a dream to become a dental hygienist and live in California one day, where it is warm. My hope is to become a citizen, so this land will be my land someday. And I'd like to be able to bring my older sister Yelda, who lives in Kabul and is lonely there, here to Maine to be with us.

More than anything, I want to grow up to be like my dad, because he was a kind person and everybody respected him for that. Even though I don't live there anymore, I care about Afghanistan, about the people there. I watch the news at night to see what is happening. It is never very optimistic. There is still war in my country, even with the U.S. helping there. There are still bombs exploding. People are still scared. My hope is for my country one day to become a peaceful land.

# I Thought I Could Fix Things

*Sara Corbett*

When I was a kid, my mother said yes to pets. We had a family dog, but for me it wasn't enough. So when, while visiting a kindergarten friend one day, I fell in love with a cat—a tiny white kitten—she let me bring the cat home, too. After that, I saved up my allowance money and my mother drove me to the mall, where I bought a couple of gerbils and a Habitrail with organ-pipe tubes and wheels for spinning, which I set up like a futuristic mini-city in my room. Sometimes the gerbils had babies and sometimes, to my horror, the adult gerbils ate those babies. Sometime later, after the gerbils had all died, I got mice. I also had a turtle named Tilly, collected from a pond one summer, who lived in a terrarium I kept near my bed, and a chameleon named Houdini who lived in another terrarium. I had an ant farm on the windowsill and spent hours watching the wasp colony that dangled outside the sill. My grandfather helped me build a cage out of chicken wire, and in it I kept a praying mantis I'd found in the garden, feeding it leaves and stalks of grass until eventually I understood this was no life for a mantis.

My white kitten grew up to be enormous and strong, a ferocious backyard hunter. A few times a week, she killed birds and little rodents and dropped their stiff bodies like offerings on the welcome mat outside our door. Because the cat belonged to me, my mother made me dispose of the corpses. I wept and said prayers as I buried them with a garden spade in one corner of our yard.

My cat got pregnant and birthed a litter of seven hairless kittens in my bedroom closet one day while I was at school. I was nine years old. I watched those kittens suckle and grow, so smitten I could hardly sleep at night. I named them and played with them and eight weeks later, as insisted upon by my mother, I put them in a box and took them to a town fair and gave them all away to strangers.

I was bereft, but my white cat, their mother, showed no emotion, resuming her nighttime prowls with renewed gusto. I'd wake sometimes to the sound of her screeching and spatting outside in the darkness beyond my window. She even killed a raccoon once, which astonished everyone in the family and, it seemed to me, made her extra smug. There were times, though, she'd only half-destroy her quarry. I'd walk outside on a fall morning and find a struggling sparrow or a maimed mole or some flailing newborn mice whose mother had been gobbled up by my cat.

Is it wrong to admit that I loved this part the most? These faltering creatures suddenly in need of care? Aware of my own limits but still striving for beatific, I administered eyedropper doses of sugar water and made mattresses of shredded Kleenex and sometimes stayed up half the night, keeping vigil and hoping the struggle would reverse itself. I once sterilized a needle with a match and gave stitches to a bleeding bird. Because—I rationalized—who else would? What I think now is that I felt thrust, in those times, into some sort of importance, the kind of thing a kid craves—a purpose in life, power. Life was all there in my bedroom and backyard—birth, death, pain, redemption—and in my makeshift set of veterinary tools. If I cared enough, I thought, I could fix things.

But really what happened was a parade of death. As I remember it, my mother never commented on what I was doing. She never interfered. I carried more dead animals to the grassy graveyard outside. I cleaned my eyedroppers and read books about veterinarians. I cried still at every loss, but I was also slowly becoming more steely, less rattled by decline. I consoled myself by imagining a billowy animal heaven, empty of predators, full of scampering rodents and soaring birds.

Decades later, just ahead of my thirtieth birthday, I went to visit a psychic. I thought it would be fun and illuminating, a way to mark the milestone. This woman came recommended by a friend. She was going to do my astrological charts and also stare somehow into my soul. I drove two hours one morning to her house in a suburb of Boston. The house was messy, but the woman seemed kind. We sat in her cluttered office, the psychic on one side of a desk with her divinings about the stars spread across it, and me on the other. At my friend's suggestion, I'd brought a tape recorder so that I could later listen to all that she'd tell me, so I'd forget none of it. The psychic told me she thought I'd been a pianist in a past life, but not a famous pianist. She told me not to worry about money. Then a dark look crossed her face. She seemed to be second-guessing herself on whether to say the next thing. But still she did. "You will know great pain," she said.

Those were the exact words. I know because it was essentially all I would remember from that day.

A couple of months later, my mother died in an accident. The news arrived in a phone call, slicing open every nerve ending, in a way that felt permanent. I wore shock like a mantle. I felt out of step with everything, overtaken by the unfairness of it. There was a perversion to the sun in the sky, to anything beautiful or regular, to people shopping for groceries or driving their cars, looking untroubled.

Grief is an exile from which you spend the rest of your life trying to return. But it is also something else. It's an initiation, a step into the bigger world.

In the months after my mother's death, I obsessed over the psychic's words. *You will know great pain.* Had she glimpsed the coming tragedy? Had she doomed me just by uttering that phrase? And worse, what was still to come? Could I check the box next to "great pain," or was there more ahead? I threw away the cassette recording of my session at the psychic's house, never wanting to hear the words again.

Because really you have no choice but to acknowledge pain and then keep living. Defiantly, stupidly, hopefully, compassionately. Every last one of us goes there and tries to come back. There is always more ahead. I understand now that life is full of small rehearsals. I know now what I was seeing as a ten-year-old kid in my own backyard, holding a white Kleenex with a dead sparrow inside. Having laid down the eyedropper, I'd pick up the garden spade, again, with my mother standing quietly nearby.

ALI MOHAMED, Hyenas
ELIZABETH GILBERT, Cheekbone

AMIRA AL SAMMRAI, Breathing in the Rain
RICHARD BLANCO, Burning in the Rain

CHRISTINA MURRAY, Carrots
JONATHAN LETHEM, Carrot-Spotting

COLIN SHEPARD, Wildernesses
BILL ROORBACH, Heat Rises

ELIAS NASRAT, The Fate of the Trees
BETSY SHOLL, That Leafless Tree

HASSAN JEYLANI, A Day in Three Worlds
CAMPBELL MCGRATH, Night and Day

JULIAN MAYORQUIN, Bottle Jacking
GEORGE SAUNDERS, Go to Jail, After Eight Times, Go Directly to Jail

RICHARD AKERA, I Started to Explain
RICHARD RUSSO, Drinking Water

VASSILY MURANGIRA, Swimming to Safety
ANN BEATTIE, Drive-by Alligator

JANET MATHIESON, A Sandwich/An Olive
ARI MEIL, Jammy Brightness

MAHAD HILOWLE, The Table
SUSAN CONLEY, The Table

DARCIE SERFES, The Bump
LILY KING, Summer

NOAH WILLIAMS, Hunting in the Deep Woods
LEWIS ROBINSON, When Dad Rode Past Me

MICHÉE RUNYAMBO, Two Teeth
MONICA WOOD, History Lesson

EMILY HOLLYDAY, Cantaloupe
GIBSON FAY-LEBLANC, Self-Portrait, with Dish Rag

MISSOURI ALICE WILLIAMS, A Little Secret
MELISSA COLEMAN, Goddess of Liberation

FADUMO ISSACK, Climbing Barefoot
JAED COFFIN, The Coconut Tree

GRACE WHITED, Box of Hope
DAVE EGGERS, Pull the Sled, Feed the Fire

AQILA SHARAFYAR, The Faithful Doves of My Father
SARA CORBETT, I Thought I Could Fix Things

ARUNA KENYI, The Photograph
MICHAEL PATERNITI, We Are Trying to Understand
What Happened to You There

# The Photograph

*Aruna Kenyi*

I am seventeen years old and I have no photographs of my past, none of my village or parents or me as a boy there, none of the places where we fled or the camps in which we lived, nor of my friends.

For instance I've never seen a picture of my oldest brother, and I will never know what he looked like. He was a captain in the army, and he was killed the year I was born: 1989. So that's why my parents gave me his name. Kenyi.

I was born in the village of Nyepo, in southern Sudan. I was one of the youngest of nine brothers and sisters. We grew corn and had chickens and goats. There were banana groves nearby and a river that ran very deep during the rainy season. I drank from that river every day and every other person born in my village drank from it, too.

My father was a farmer. He had a very calm voice. That's what I remember. He never went to school, just grew the food to help his family survive. He was also a soldier, and once after he accidentally dropped his rifle in the water, they put him in prison.

I'm told that I'm tall like him, but look more like my mother. She had lots of hair—and was really fast. If I did something wrong and tried to run away, she always caught me.

My village was happiness. That's what I remember. And Christmas was the best day of the year. All the families played together, to all hours of the night. We ate bananas and played drums. We made guns out of branches and acted like we were soldiers, too. We hid and captured each other in the banana grove. Some of us pretended we were children, and some pretended we were parents.

I will tell you now about the night everything changed. It was the hour just after dinner when families go to visit each other. Everybody gets up and wanders from place to place, saying their hellos. My tribe, the Bari—we're very friendly people. I was with three of my brothers, playing. I would have been five years old. Meanwhile, my parents had gone to our garden, to pick corn.

That's when the Arab militia attacked. Everything was peaceful, and then I heard a noise like an earthquake. I saw the plane coming, and they started bombing our village, and then they came in trucks. The soldiers were yelling at us to leave our homes, and they started killing people and burning everything.

Of course, everyone ran in a different direction to save his or her life. Some mothers and fathers even forgot their kids. That's how I was separated from my parents. My brother led us into a cane field and we hid there for the night. We could see the fires and hear the screaming. There were many mosquitoes and the grass was sharp and wet on my face.

In the morning there was nothing left. No houses, nothing. My oldest brother, who was twenty at the time, said, "It's no use. Our parents are probably dead, and we don't want to die here, too," so we got up from the field and started walking. "I'd rather die ahead," he said.

I just wanted my parents, that's all I remember. From that point on my life has been one of never getting to say good-bye.

So we walked for a year, through different tribal lands: the Koko, the Mari. Some were friendly; some were not. It was very far for a young boy, and my brothers sometimes carried me. We ended up in a camp in Uganda called Kali. There were many lost children—and a lot of disease and death. It was here that we met my uncle and where he was shot and stoned when Ugandan rebels attacked. They burned houses with people in them, like before, and we ran again and hid in the fields by the mountains.

During this time I thought about my mother and father. I could remember them taking care of us. We would have a bath every night. I was a really bad kid, so they were always having to punish me. When I was hungry, my mother would say, "If you don't want to work, then there's no food for you today." These were the lessons I learned.

Sometimes my brothers would tell stories about them and when they did, it made me believe that my parents were not dead, like they were here again with us.

Later, we ended up in the camp at Kyangwali. We stayed there five years. I remember it was next to a forest and the monkeys and baboons scared me. I didn't have time for homework. I worked our little garden all the time to try and get food—corn, beans, and nuts. Like my father had once.

And then one day they told us to get ready, that we were going to America.

We'd spent years hoping for this moment, and then when it came, we had no time to say good-bye to anyone, none of our good friends, no one. They just put us on a truck and took us to the airport. We left many people there. We flew from Kampala to Nairobi to the UK to New York to Virginia, where we lived for the first year. Then we came to Portland.

We were lucky, my brothers and I. We survived all those years without illness or real harm. We grew up without parents, which was very hard. Every night, in those camps, we'd have to wait two or three hours on line for water because the big people just kept pushing past us. There was no one to protect us.

Not long after coming to Portland we had a letter in the mail, and in that letter, was . . . a photograph! I don't know how to say this, but it was of my mother and father. They were alive. My mother was standing and my father was sitting in a wheelchair because the soldiers shot his legs off. They looked so old—my father's hair was gray—but I remember looking at that photograph for a very long time. I've since talked to my father on the phone in Sudan. His voice is like I remember it: calm. But he has had a hard life. He said he would like to go back to our village someday, but right now I won't let him.

All of our happiness was there—and it's still not possible to return.

# We Are Trying to Understand What Happened to You There

*Michael Paterniti*

He's sixteen, and doesn't have a single photograph from his past. Not of his parents or siblings, nor the village or his friends there. He only has pictures in his head, he says. And he wants to get them out. In order that everyone else might see.

\* \* \*

He's a junior in high school, dressed in a white, collared shirt, with a gold cross dangling around his neck. He's nervous and shy—and keeps calling you "sir," even after you've repeated that it's okay if he uses your first name, until you start calling *him* sir. Then his eyes flash, his cheeks rise, and he breaks into a blinding smile.

\* \* \*

He hesitates and stumbles at first, whether it's nerves, or just the flood of things he wants to say as the words fail him, English being his fourth language. But eventually, he takes a deep breath. Outside, it's gray and snowing in his new home by the sea, windows scrimshawed by ice—and he says, "I was born in a hot, dusty place where the river ran deep in the rainy season." Like he's beginning a poem, or a fairytale. And then it all comes pouring out, until you realize it's not a fairytale at all.

\* \* \*

He remembers being the youngest of nine. There were chickens and goats. He drank each day from a river that ran near the village. He remembers eating bananas, and how Christmas was the best day of the year, when people brought out their drums. Then the dancing went late into the night, voices raised in joy, the drums pounding like a heartbeat.

\* \* \*

He ate corn and drank from the same river. His mother and father were there, and his eight siblings. They played in the banana grove, until his father called him back home, with that calm voice of his. And his mother gave him a bath.

\* \* \*

There's a beast loose in the world. It seeks to devour whatever appears in its path, including the least culpable among us. Afterward, we conduct our forensics. We gather the bones, trace back the footsteps, compile the facts. We try to understand what happened to the innocents there, to inoculate ourselves. Or to prepare for the moment when it comes for us.

\* \* \*

He was playing after dinner, when the bombing began. He ran to a cane field with his brothers, and lay on his stomach, in hiding. Through the leaves, he could see flames devouring the village. The next morning he rose with his brothers and started walking, following a line of boys that kept growing across southern Sudan. He was five years old at the time. He left with only the clothes he wore—and walked this way for a year.

\* \* \*

Some days walking across the south of the country, you find there's no food. Some days you have to ford a river with crocodiles. Some days you're so hot and exhausted, your brother lifts you from the ground and carries you in his arms, until he puts you down again, for he, too, hasn't eaten.

\* \* \*

They walked this way for a year, then spent many more in various refugee camps, believing their parents to be dead. Telling it now, he sometimes loses track of how many years in each location. They jumble in his mind. He smiles, a little embarrassed by his own confusion. He thinks he should know these facts and dates, but he was young, and so afraid of monkeys. His uncle was killed in one camp, when rebels attacked. Disease was rampant. "It's a miracle," he says, "that worse things didn't happen to us."

\* \* \*

You find your ways to survive: the little garden plot, a prayer at night, a story that works. You stand in line for two or three hours, waiting for a jug of water, dreaming that you're drinking again from the river in your village.

\* \* \*

He tells this story over and over—about the bombing and the walk, the camps and how he eventually came to America, land of many cereal boxes. It's hard to imagine so much having happened to a sixteen-year-old, but it's just his life. When he retells it, he wears that polite smile, so as not to cause you any discomfort.

\* \* \*

The photograph eventually arrives through the mail, of his father in a wheelchair with no legs—and his mother standing behind. He's buried them in his mind, and here they are, broken but risen again. But it's not clear what you do with a loss like this: some drink it away, some try to reimagine it, marshal it, and carry on with a deeper sense of purpose.

In the case of the boy, he keeps writing—dozens upon dozens of pages— until an e-mail arrives in your inbox. "Let me know when we're going to meet again, sir," he writes, "so I can hand you this book I've finished."

\* \* \*

He has written a book. It's his autobiography. It's taken him two years. English is his fourth language, and the book, a couple hundred pages, is written in English. When you walk across a country, then survive ten years in limbo, anything must seem possible.

"Sir," he says at his book party, "I know this will sound weird, but I'm already writing a Part Two."

\* \* \*

We are trying to understand what happened to you there. And you are trying to tell us, over and over again. In a perfect world, this is how it should work: You speak—and we listen, as if it happened to us.

\* \* \*

Each time he tells his story, the houses, which are thatched huts, rise from their ashes. You can see the goats and cows in the fields, and taste the corn for dinner. His father's voice calls to him in the banana grove, and when he hears it, he runs home on five-year-old legs. The story is the river you both drink from.

Standing before you, he fiddles with his gold cross—and smiles. He's telling you about the drums at Christmas, how they beat all night into dawn. When you're a boy, you believe they will never stop. And they never do, even all these years later, in the faraway country you now call home.

They wake you in the middle of the night, sometimes with a start of fear—and after you find your own heartbeat again, they put you back to sleep.

# WRITERS ON WRITING

*Describe an early moment when you thought you might be a writer.*

RICHARD AKERA:

The answer to *why write* is simple. I write because I find it comforting and enjoyable at the same time. *Why share?* Why not? Why write if you are not going to share? I feel like if I share my story with people, somehow someone out there will relate to my story and maybe it will help them in one way or another.

MELISSA COLEMAN:

Since childhood, stories and books have helped me better understand the world, and so it seemed only natural to try to write stories in order to better understand life.

SARA CORBETT:

In my town, when you turned six, you were old enough to have your own library card. The day I got my library card changed everything. It was literally the key to the kingdom. The library gave me permission to be curious. Over time, I carried home piles of books—about insects, about the Ganges River, about Mars. I could read one Nancy Drew mystery and then go back and take out the next. It was a revelation! It was a bottomless, inexhaustible place, my hometown library, and it helped me understand something similar about the world, too. Words connected me to all that I didn't know. They were like a river current you could ride into any frontier. I don't think I thought I could be a writer, exactly, but from that time on, I knew I wanted somehow to take that ride.

GIBSON FAY-LEBLANC:

It depends what you mean by *early*. Growing up, I loved to read and could write serviceably well for school, but I had no idea that being a writer was even possible. I mostly went to Catholic school, and there was no such thing as creative writing with the nuns. I left for college thinking I'd go to medical school and did well in my science courses the first few years. It wasn't until my senior year that I took a poetry class with Christopher Merrill and wrote some terrible poems. But I loved doing it. I ended up writing and giving a speech at my graduation—that was my first experience with writing something and having an audience be moved by it. I was hooked.

ELIZABETH GILBERT:

I never remember for a moment wanting to be anything else (except briefly, in eighth grade, when I decided for a spell that I wanted to be a chiropractor, for reasons that are now completely lost to history). I do remember clearly the moment that I decided to give my life to writing—almost the way you would join a holy order. I was about sixteen years old, and I simply committed to it. I made a pact that I would not stop writing until I was dead, no matter what the outcome. (And people in my family live a really long time, so this was a serious commitment!) The contract I made to the universe went something like this: "I can't promise that I will write good books, but I promise that I will write books. The best I can, for as long as I can." I also promised that I would do whatever it took to support myself materially or financially, but would never stop writing. It has made my life simple, holding on to the terms of this pact. When everything else has gone screwy or sideways in my life, I have held to that promise firmly. It is the immovable rock at the center of my whole self.

FADUMO ISSACK:

I first thought I would be a writer when I was in the refugee camp. My passion for writing began there. When my parents told me stories about their childhood and their homeland, I would picture what it had been like for them. I wanted to capture those moments and write them down. Also some moments I wished to write down were about what was going on in Somalia, as our histories are passed down orally only, at least in some families. Our family was one of those. I wanted to be the first one to write it all down.

ARUNA KENYI:

The first moment that I thought I was going to be a writer was when The Telling Room visited my high school art classroom and invited others and me to join their writing program.

JONATHAN LETHEM:

The "aha" moment for me was when I first gathered that *Alice in Wonderland* and *Through the Looking Glass* were loaded with puns, puzzles, linguistic jokes, and parodies of other writings. In that instant, "Lewis Carroll" existed for me in the most extraordinary way, as a presence, an intelligence behind the text, making it all happen. And I immediately wanted to be "that guy."

VASSILY MURANGIRA:

I started by being a reader. I never saw myself writing stories before, but The Telling Room helped to discover the other side of me I never knew that I had. I wrote my first piece when I was working with The Telling Room to see if I could, and I did well enough to encourage myself to carry on and write another.

CHRISTINA MURRAY:

*The Bell Jar* by Sylvia Plath was the first book that inspired me to write. Any work by Plath still inspires me today. Also, Toni Morrison has become an author who has inspired me to try to write prose again. The way she combines social issues and the everyday experience really amazes me.

MICHAEL PATERNITI:

My mom used to read a book to my brothers and me when we were kids, called *Randy's Dandy's Lions*. It was about a lion tamer who couldn't control his crazy lions at the circus. Man, I loved that book! It was so funny and chaotic and great. I made my mom read it to me again and again. I think that's where it started, with a question: Why is this book so cool? Which later became: Wouldn't it be cool to make something like that?

BILL ROORBACH:

I asked a department-store Santa for a desk when I was five. My mother asked me why I wanted a desk. I said I wanted to be a writer. No idea where that came from!

MICHÉE RUNYAMBO:

The earliest moment I thought I was writer was when I was holding The Telling Room's book, *Exit 13*. I was reading my story to my little sister and looking at her eyes and saw how she was lost in the story, in *my* story. I think that's when I realized I was a writer.

GEORGE SAUNDERS:

A nun—a particularly "hot" nun, I might add—gave me a copy of *Johnny Tre-maine* with the warning that it was a hard book and might be too much for me, etc. This was intriguing. And when I read it, and got it, I went around for weeks thinking in the language of that book—a form of "being a writer," I guess.

BETSY SHOLL:

I always wanted to write, even when I was in third grade and thought that might mean writing book reports with illustrations for the rest of my life. In fourth grade, I kept a tiny blue spiral notebook with terrible poems in it, which I made everybody in my family listen to. I was a stutterer, so writing was a way of being fluent, of being able to use the words I loved. There were a lot of rules in my family about what we should and shouldn't say, so writing was a way of giving myself a voice.

GRACE WHITED:

One event that made me think of becoming an author was in kindergarten, when my class had an author's tea. My teacher encouraged all of the students to write their own stories and share them with the class. Our writing was typed and bound, and we were allowed to illustrate our books. I can still remember the exhilaration of sharing my writing with an audience for the first time. A second memorable moment was when I was seven, and the entire first grade was encouraged to write stories and drop them off in a box, and each week your story would come back typed up and ready to be illustrated. Every time I saw my name on a book, it was the best feeling in the world, and that's when I really knew I wanted to be an author.

MISSOURI ALICE WILLIAMS:

I started writing when I was six years old, and to this day I love to write. I always thought about being a writer, but never really thought about pursuing it as a career.

***Which book(s) inspired you early on, and what books still inspire you or have most recently inspired you?***

RICHARD AKERA:

Early on, I didn't read at all, except when we scratched a few letters in the dirt with a stick, before the bigger kids crawled all over us to reach the food line when the government meal came. School was not an option for me. I learned to read when I was fifteen, in the refugee camp in Kampala, Uganda. Today I have two library cards and I read two or three books a week. It's the best. I choose whatever I like. I loved Randy Pausch's *The Last Lecture*. It's so uplifting, and it's about life. Right now I'm reading *To Kill a Mockingbird*. Recently I read *The Great Gatsby*. I have no words for that book, but the book has words for me. This is one of my favorite quotes; I like to believe that I relate to it one way or the other: "Whenever you feel like criticizing anyone…just remember that all the people in this world haven't had the advantages that you've had."

JAED COFFIN:
*Hatchet*, by Gary Paulsen, was huge. *On the Road* was my first love. *Notes of a Native Son* is what I go back to when I lose track of what I'm doing.

SUSAN CONLEY:
I read poetry in college and in graduate school. I devoured poetry books the way you might speed through Agatha Christie mystery novels. Poetry is the distillation. It is the way to say it new. Poetry held secrets that it was willing to whisper to me when I was twenty. I came of age in the 1980s reading Elizabeth Bishop and Anne Sexton and Sylvia Plath, who all reigned in poetry workshops across the United States. The next generation of women poets—Sharon Olds, Carolyn Forche, Jorie Graham, and Louise Gluck—was where I really fell in love with the compression of the narrative. Then I got more and more interested in the interrupted narrative and the cross-pollination of genres. Now I'm fascinated at where one genre blends and morphs into another and how artificial that gap can be, for example, between a long, narrative poem and a memoir or novel.

SARA CORBETT:
Wow, where to start? *Charlotte's Web*, the stories of Hans Christian Andersen, the Sherlock Holmes collection by Sir Arthur Conan Doyle, *A Wrinkle in Time*, and everything by James Herriot. The book that revolutionized my life, though, was *The White Album* by Joan Didion, which my mother gave me as a gift when I was in high school. There were so few women writing narrative nonfiction—or at least being recognized for doing it—and to a teenage girl who wanted to write, and who wanted the adventure of journalism, it meant everything to me to read Didion, a master of the craft above all the male masters, and to feel that it was possible.

ELIZABETH GILBERT:

The Wizard of Oz series by L. Frank Baum. This is my origin story. I grew up with well-worn copies of these books—books that had been handed down through my family for several generations, complete with their stunning Art Deco illustrations. The Oz stories were tales of a farm girl (which I was) who went on otherworldly adventures (which I wanted to do) and who was incredibly brave (which I still want to be). I always credit these books with making me into a traveler and a writer. If you have an especially dreamy little girl in your house, forget about Disney videos; get her a boxed set of these books.

EMILY HOLLYDAY:

For laughs, I used to read *The Seven Silly Eaters,* but now I go to David Sedaris. *The Lupine Lady* inspired me when I was young, and recently Terry Tempest Williams has prompted me to reflect and envision the years ahead of me.

ARUNA KENYI:

*What is the What* by Dave Eggers is the book that inspired me to write more, and meeting Valentino Achak Deng when he came to town with the author for The Telling Room also made writing intriguing to me.

ARI MEIL:

In high school I had to write a report covering multiple books by a single author. I picked Kurt Vonnegut, and though I wasn't much of a reader until then, I ended up reading about a dozen of his novels for the report despite only being required to read five. I return annually to these books and read a few at a time. It helps me remember the effect a funny, unconventional, honest sci-fi writer can have on the world. Another book that has stuck with me through the years is *Coming Through Slaughter,* by Michael Ondaatje. Its intense and unpretentious mix of poetic prose, primary-source historical documents, and streaming narrative made me realize just how few rules there really are to telling a great story. It remains one of the most hard-core and eye-opening books I've ever encountered.

CHRISTINA MURRAY:

My creative writing teacher in high school is really the one who opened my eyes to the fact that I could be a writer. Before taking her class, I had never tried writing, but she pushed me to try every form of writing, and that is how I found that I had a knack for poetry. She helped me find an outlet for everything I had to say.

MICHAEL PATERNITI:

I loved all those adventure books: *King Arthur, Swiss Family Robinson, Robin Hood, Treasure Island*. I remember in middle school being forced to read an essay by Thoreau, and in it there was a description of ice that was so startling and beautiful I could hardly believe it. I remember reading about Ichabod Crane and then going to Sleepy Hollow itself, which tied the story to a real place. Today, I usually read *The Great Gatsby, To the Lighthouse*, and *Lolita* every so often to remind myself what greatness is. I just read a Finnish novel called *The Howling Miller* that kind of blew me away. And that's still the most amazing feeling.

BILL ROORBACH:

Lately I have been finding music to be most inspirational. Charles Mingus on YouTube, for example, "Moanin." Wow!

BETSY SHOLL:

I loved A. A. Milne as a kid. Then in college I discovered William Carlos Williams and Yeats. After that, Sylvia Plath blew my mind, and Elizabeth Bishop sort of calmed and deepened it. At one point Denis Johnson was hugely important to me. Right now I read Osip Mandelstam, Czeslaw Milosz, W. G. Sebald, Wislawa Szymborska, and Adam Zagajewski over and over—those writers who have had to face the darkest elements of the twentieth century. I recently became a fan of Laura Kasischke. I always come back to Brigit Kelly and Bishop—and I read Dante every few years, spending 100 days reading a canto a day, from hell to paradise.

GRACE WHITED:

Very early on, the Junie B. Jones series inspired me in my kindergarten years. My teacher would read the books to my class, and my mother would read them to me at home. In fact, I was so inspired, I cut my friend's hair just like Junie B. Jones. Let's just say it didn't go over as well with my teacher as I thought it would. Currently, the Divergent series by Veronica Roth is a powerful inspiration to me. It is a huge hit with the young population, and the way she writes is captivating. Veronica Roth also takes her plot in directions that many authors don't dare to do, breaking out of the boundaries, which I especially love about her books. I hope to take my writing in new, unique directions like all of my favorite authors.

MISSOURI ALICE WILLIAMS:

The book that inspired me to start writing was *Good Poems*, by Garrison Keillor. When I was young, my family and I would read a poem every night after dinner. Listening to other poets' words and the way they wrote their poems gave me ideas and made me want to start writing my own.

NOAH WILLIAMS:

The book that catalyzed my interest in writing was a copy of *The Complete Short Stories of Ernest Hemingway: The Finca Vigia Edition*. Reading for the first time how Francis Macomber lost his life on safari and the adventures of Nick Adams completely fascinated me, and eventually gave me the framework to start my own short stories. *Cathedral*, *Officer Friendly*, and *Tarantula* were inspiring reads as well.

MONICA WOOD:

I just reread the works of J. D. Salinger, whom I discovered in high school. His work was transforming for me, because I didn't realize it was permitted to write the way people actually talked. I really didn't. I started writing imitation Salinger after that, and eventually found my own way. The stories still feel fresh and contemporary to me, even though they were written before I was born.

**Which teacher or mentor was especially important to your development as a writer? Why?**

RICHARD BLANCO:

Mr. Panzer, my senior English teacher. He made language come alive.

JAED COFFIN:

My art teacher at Brunswick High School, Donna Coffin (no relation), taught me that art is four-fifths seeing and one-fifth drawing, that to observe an object carefully is more important than being able to reproduce it on paper. I think that's why I write nonfiction. It forces me to rely on actual realities of the world rather than skate by on mere glances or assumptions.

MELISSA COLEMAN:

My parents have both given me some of the most vital material to write about (as a memoirist), and also taught me the most about how to live—how to work hard, persevere, and be grateful—and that's led me to want to capture these learnings by writing about them.

SARA CORBETT:

My seventh-grade English teacher, Gary Hendrikson, was the most impassioned teacher I ever had. He loved books and would practically leap around the room as we discussed them in class. He was *present*. He was the first person in my life to build a bridge between the reading I did at home and the learning we did in the classroom. And maybe most important of all, one day he had a real-life novelist—a local guy—come visit our class and talk about being a writer. This became another bridge for me, seeing that the words I so often revered on the page originated from a living, breathing human being—that writing was not so removed from my everyday world.

DAVE EGGERS:

I had a pretty much uninterrupted string of great teachers growing up, and they all encouraged me greatly. I made my first book in first grade with Mrs. Wright, and made another with Ms. Dunn in fifth grade, and other in eighth grade with Mrs. Dristle. When I got to high school, I had a group of truly extraordinary teachers who were very professorial in their methods and set an incredible example. Mr. Benton, Mr. Ferry, Mrs. Lowey, Mr. Hawkins, and Mr. Criche were all unforgettable influences.

ARUNA KENYI:

My high school art teacher was the first person who helped me develop my writing. She had each student in her classroom pick and work on a project of their choice. I chose to write about my journey to the U.S. and drew pictures that went along with the story. That project turned into "The Photograph," which then led me to write my own book, *Between Two Rivers*.

JULIAN MAYORQUIN:

Debbie Duffet pushed me educationally in every direction. She didn't allow me to quit or give up. She was in the navy and really instilled that "do not quit" attitude in her students.

MICHAEL PATERNITI:

I wonder if it's true that most writers can look back and connect the dots between a lot of mentors and teachers, each of whom gave them some little gift in the exact moment they most needed it. Sometimes, too, it has nothing to do with writing. My middle school English teacher taught me to pay attention—really pay attention!—to what I was reading and let it elevate me. I had a high school teacher who thought I plagiarized something, which made me think, "Maybe I'm a little better at this than she thinks I am." I had a swim coach who yelled at me a lot, and sometimes when I'm sitting at my desk, convinced I have nothing to say, I can hear his voice, screaming, "What the hell are you doing, Paterniti . . . SWIM!!"

LEWIS ROBINSON:
Which teacher or mentor was especially important to your development as a writer? Why? In college, as I was getting more obsessed with reading and writing short stories, I had a teacher named Jay Parini who said to me, "You know, this is something you could do." He wasn't standing on a desk and he didn't say it with a lot of fanfare, but it was absolutely amazing to hear. Of course, I didn't fully believe him—my stories, honestly, were imitative and lackluster—but I was encouraged enough by what he'd said to continue practicing.

BILL ROORBACH:
One teacher in college said I'd never be a writer. I pretty much owe him my career.

GEORGE SAUNDERS:
I had two high school teachers (Joe and Sheri Lindbloom) who saw something in me and encouraged me to write down little "insights" I was having in class—which was a huge thing, this idea that *my words* might contain power. And then later they helped get me into college by calling the college and pleading my case: "Yes, his grades are terrible, but he is ready to start trying, and we think he can do it." God bless them.

GRACE WHITED:
One teacher who contributed to my development as a writer was my kindergarten teacher, Mrs. Thompson. She taught me how to read and write, and hosted an author's tea, where she had each student write a story and read it out loud to the class. Currently, two of the most influential mentors for me are Marilyn and Djelloul Marbrook, who are both authors. They have guided and supported my passion for writing, sending me the works of both classic and modern authors and contributing greatly to the development of my craft.

Missouri Alice Williams:

I still listen to Garrison Keillor often on the radio and have recently been look-ing at some new books to help me improve my writing. My parents are both big writers, so when I was starting out they were mentors, helping me develop and gain more knowledge about writing.

Noah Williams:

There are three people who without a doubt have made me the writer I am today. Leslie Appelbaum was the first person who ever gave me professional direction and feedback on my writing and is now my A.P. English teacher and continues to challenge me in my writing. Eliza Lambert was my first and best peer editor. She edited the piece included in this anthology, and it was Eliza who pushed me to enter the 2010 writing contest in the first place. And Derek Pierce, who is quite the writer himself, fed me the books and authors that helped me develop into the writer I am today.

Monica Wood:

My sister Anne was my high school English teacher, the best teacher I ever had. She did not tolerate slipshod writing, but was quick with praise when I did things right. (She also gave me the only *B* I ever got in English!)

### *Describe your ideal space/time/location in which to write.*

Richard Akera:

I tend to think best when I'm in the shower and when I wake up in the middle of the night. I know this might sound crazy to some, but sometimes I take a notebook and a pen with me to the bathroom so that I don't forget the one good idea that comes to me in the shower. When I wake up in the middle of the night, I sometimes write for an hour or two before going back to bed.

Amira Al Sammrai:

A quiet place, such as my room, is a good place to write and get out all the emotion that I have inside. The ideal time for me is at night, because night is always quiet.

Richard Blanco:

At night, I'm a vampire writer. I like to write when the whole world is quiet and I feel like I'm doing the mystery work of the world . . .

JAED COFFIN:

Between 10 P.M. and 2 A.M., when I'm—sadly—far away from my family, in some town where I don't know anyone. Or, from 6 A.M. to 10 A.M. in the room where I grew up at my mom's house.

SUSAN CONLEY:

In order to slide into the prose dream, it's a great thing if I can rise in the morning and go directly to the page: Do not pass Go. Do not collect $200. (We play a fair bit of Monopoly in our house.) But the real culprit is the Internet. It can be the death of a good writing day. So often we may say that we will write just one important e-mail. Hours later, we are still writing e-mails or trolling the Internet doing "book research." The research, I have come to learn from too much experience, can always wait. I write in a little writing room in our old attic, and it suits me well to be up there quite alone but with a tether to the real world.

SARA CORBETT:

Five-thirty in the morning, two cups of coffee into the day, before anyone else in the house is awake, and as far away from the Internet as possible.

GIBSON FAY-LEBLANC:

In the morning, in a quiet house, with a cup of coffee or tea. With two young sons, that doesn't happen very often right now, though some mornings, if I can kind of hold the world at an arm's length—no social media, no e-mail, no news—once the boys are on the school bus, I can return to that quiet house, and it's not half bad.

EMILY HOLLYDAY:

The best time for me to write is right after I have gone for a run. I become so bored running that I make up a story to keep me going. The stories are usually based on something that I saw, heard, or experienced and can only process in narrative form.

FADUMO ISSACK:

My ideal space to write is a quiet place where I can focus, such as a library or in my room. My ideal time to write is at night when everybody is sleeping.

ARUNA KENYI:

When I was in high school, I wrote my story in my room at home, at The Telling Room, and sometimes at the Portland Public Library. While in college, I did my writing at the computer center.

JONATHAN LETHEM:

For me, always, the first thing in the morning, before I've entered the social matrix of conversations, e-mails, encounters, responsibilities. Ideally, I'll get up before anyone else in the house and creep off into some corner with a cup of coffee. Most recently, I've been writing in a walk-in closet, outfitted with a special computer with no Internet on it. That works very nicely.

CAMPBELL MCGRATH:

I think it's important to maintain flexibility in one's writing process—not to become too concretized in one's practice. But I do know that what works best for me is to write early in the day, like all morning into early afternoon. And then, to read through the day's work at bedtime, making some final revisions, etc. In the morning, when back at the desk, I not only have my revisions to get me started, I have all the great dream-work my mind has been doing while I slept. I have solved countless problems in my poems while dead asleep. Give your mind a task to perform while your consciousness turns off, and there's a good chance it will get done.

ARI MEIL:

Whenever I have more than thirty minutes to spare and a surface to sit on.

VASSILY MURANGIRA:

It's always hard to find enough time for all the things we want to do. But some-how it's extra-difficult to find writing time, especially when you are a student and have tons of homework and other things to do. But I usually find myself writing late at night, when it's calm and no one is around me. That's when I can focus on my work.

CHRISTINA MURRAY:

There are long periods of time in which I suffer from insomnia, so most of my writing takes place in the middle of the night, usually outside if weather per-mits. I don't mind writing in the middle of the night; in fact, I usually prefer it because that is the only time when I have absolute quiet.

BILL ROORBACH:
I used to be fussier. Now just any little block of time that presents itself any-where works great.

GEORGE SAUNDERS:
I wrote my first book at work, so my standards for when and where to write got pretty low. I wrote parts of it on the bus, late at night, when I was supposed to be writing a technical report. So mostly for me, now, it has to do with feeling happy—ideally, I like to work when I feel kind of free and revved up. But writ-ing will also gradually make me feel free and revved up.

MISSOURI ALICE WILLIAMS:
I like to write my poems during the day, when I can listen to people talk and observe my surroundings.

## Why write, and why share what you write?

AMIRA AL SAMMRAI:
I like to write because I want to get everything inside me out on paper. Most of the time writing helps broken people to heal, dispelling what's hurting them. Sharing what I'm writing keeps me motivated to write more and more, and it makes me feel that my work is reaching people.

RICHARD BLANCO:
I write to learn something new about the world and about myself and about others. I share it because I hope whoever reads it will learn something new about the world and themselves and others.

ELIZABETH GILBERT:
I write for the delight of it. I know this isn't very German Romantic of me, but I enjoy the big magic of writing. This doesn't mean writing is easy, but it does mean I find it interesting, and I like to be interested better than anything. I like puzzling through a project. I like that marvelous and strange sense of intersect-ing my human efforts with the weirdo mysteries of creativity. And I share my work for the same reason I think people should share most things—to delight the world and not be greedy or too self-serious or hoarding. I did an interview once with Tom Waits in which he said, "All I do, as a musician, is make jewelry for the inside of people's minds." I love this approach—that art is not neces-

sarily the most grandiose or important thing in the world, that the stakes are not necessarily so high as we creators sometimes imagine them to be . . . that, really, all we are doing is crafting jewelry for the inside of people's heads. What a wonderful job description!

EMILY HOLLYDAY:

Why write? Writing has helped me feel empathy and compassion for the characters that I create. I can also understand reality better once I have written about it. Why share? Because stories are an amazing way to follow someone's voice into his or her imagination and way of thinking.

ARUNA KENYI:

I decided to document my story to help others in the community at large learn about my culture, beliefs, and the reasons I left my country.

JULIAN MAYORQUIN:

A story worth telling should always make its way onto paper.

CAMPBELL MCGRATH:

Writers write for many reasons, from the mundane to the cosmic. Some of my reasons for writing poetry are:

a)   Art is fun. For me, writing poetry is the grown-up equivalent of finger painting.
b)   The close engagement with language that is at the heart of poetry is a fantastic challenge, or encounter, or wrestling match; when the writing is going well, the poet and the language are like the sperm whale and the giant squid, fighting out in the deepest trenches of the Pacific Ocean.
c)   It keeps me off the streets.

ARI MEIL:

I think that the answers to these questions are the most important things any writer can figure out if they want to make great work. I'm still looking for satisfactory answers for myself.

VASSILY MURANGIRA:

I write because I like writing, and I share what I write because I like to be read by other people. Otherwise, what would be the reason to write?

Lewis Robinson:

I have a lot of depressing moments at my desk when I feel incapable of describing something or simply not talented enough to make a story work. But I've finally gotten to the point where I know I can bulldoze my way past those moments of doubt, keep my head down, and produce some sentences and paragraphs and chapters that feel alive to me. It's more of an addiction than anything else.

Bill Roorbach:

I just want to be loved.

Michée Runyambo:

I'm a very quiet person. I like to keep things to myself, but throughout my whole life, I've been through war and seen a lot of good and bad things, and I needed to find a way to release either my pain or my joy. Writing seems to be the perfect medication for me.

Richard Russo:

For me, writing is thinking. It's *how* I think, more than *what*. Writing forces me to slow down and test my opinions and perceptions and experiences for truth. Things I say in casual conversation just disappear, which makes me happy, because most of it doesn't deserve repeating or remembering. To commit something to print is to believe it more deeply, to be willing to defend it. We've all been surprised to hear certain things come out of our own mouths, things we never thought we believed until we said them. With writing, this happens all the time. I don't write to tell people what I think, but rather to discover what I think.

Betsy Sholl:

I think we all have to ask ourselves this question again and again, and the answers are multiple and changing. There is some urge to write that is perhaps beyond having a reason, the desire to shape something in words, to respond to the world's beauty, or its terror, its sorrow or joy—some need to take stock, to give back. It may be the same urge that causes us to sigh, or gasp or laugh—the world striking a chord, which then resonates back. After a while it becomes part of who one is, woven into the fabric of life, so one keeps going, always wanting to write something more beautiful, more accurate, more true or challenging than the thing before, which reveals its flaws as soon as it's done . . . As to sharing, I guess after one's worked for a good while, revising and shaping a piece of writing, it just needs to be sent out, given away. Otherwise the pipeline gets clogged. There is also a sense of having to let go, to place the work under a larger scrutiny, so it doesn't become precious. As in all life, letting go is a necessary part of the process.

GEORGE SAUNDERS:

Mostly I think we write because we enjoy it. That's sure true for me. It makes me feel more alive, aware, confident, and more sympathetic toward other people. It is also (or can be) a healthy way of asserting one's self in the world— getting a little power, growing into one's individuality. And, at the highest level, it breaks down, or at least softens, the border separating "us" from "everything else."

GRACE WHITED:

The reason I love writing is because it is the purest form of my innermost thoughts and feelings. When I write, it helps me clear my mind, and I feel like I can truly be myself in my writing, with no filters or judgment from the outside world. The reason I want to share what I write is because I want to bring happiness to other people. I also want to touch my readers' hearts the way my favorite authors touch mine. If I could become influential to a future generation, that would mean the world to me.

MISSOURI ALICE WILLIAMS:

Writing poetry, I think, is a great way to let your imagination go wild, but also an interesting way to express your thoughts and feelings on paper. I think the best way to become a better writer is by sharing it with the world and letting other people see your writing and how it may be different from how others write.

# ON THE WRITING PROCESS

*What do you write on—paper, computer, or both? (Napkins count as paper.)*

AMIRA AL SAMMRAI:
When I write on paper, I feel that I want to write more and more, because paper makes me continue writing without limits. Paper sometimes helps me get out all my ideas, what feelings I have in my heart, and what thinking is going on in my mind. Paper allows me to write without being worried about my grammar and my English limitations, and especially without the distraction of the red line shown underneath every misspelled word.

DAVE EGGERS:
I take notes on paper, then put it all together on a laptop.

GIBSON FAY-LEBLANC:
I keep a notebook filled with ideas, story/poem ideas, lines, things overheard or seen or smelled, etc. Fairly early on in the process, I go to the computer and then do all my revising and editing there.

FADUMO ISSACK:
What I write on is whatever is available to me at the moment. I remember writing on trees, on the ground, in the sand. When I first learned to write I wrote on a chalkboard with black ink. I write on computer and paper, both of them.

ARUNA KENYI:
When I first started writing, I used to write on a notebook and then type it up on a computer, but now I just type it onto a computer instead of writing in notebooks.

JULIAN MAYORQUIN:
I am a product of this age and stick to typing.

CAMPBELL MCGRATH:
Most of my poems begin in a journal or notebook and are then whipped into shape on the computer. There's a nice balance between the computer's clean, graphic presentation of words in space and the organic sense of words written by hand. So it goes, back and forth: print out a copy of a new draft, scrawl all over it, input changes, print again.

ARI MEIL:
I write exclusively on my computer. When I am in the flow, working the keys feels like playing an instrument, and the avalanche of keystrokes energizes me and contributes to the joy of writing for me.

VASSILY MURANGIRA:
When I am writing, I use my computer, I think it's easier that way because I save my work and whenever I have time again, I can go back and keep adding more ideas.

BILL ROORBACH:
I write on the computer now, mostly. I can barely hold a pencil anymore!

BETSY SHOLL:
I write in notebooks, by hand, and sort of hide early drafts, as if maybe they'll magically turn into something better if I just leave them. For me it's a mistake to move too quickly. I don't move to the computer until the writing has sat a good while in that notebook with various added scribbles.

GRACE WHITED:
I started out writing on paper, but transitioned to the computer because it was easier to edit and save my work without cluttering up my room. Although the computer is more efficient, I do miss writing on paper occasionally because it is the most traditional way of writing. There's something in the way you can look at twenty pages of your handwriting and think "I did all of this" that instills a sort of pride in you. But when I get an idea, it doesn't matter what I write on—napkins, my iPhone, sometimes even my own hand—as long as I get the idea down.

MISSOURI ALICE WILLIAMS:

When I write, I always start with paper and pen. Then, once I feel confident with what I have written, I will go to the computer and type it up.

***When putting ideas to words, do you work from notes or an outline? Do you do much research?***

SUSAN CONLEY:

I like to write in notebooks. This is the chicken-scrawl, first idea, first bad draft stuff. These paragraphs may include some rough outlines and some macro thinking on a novel idea or on some key moment in a book I'm working on. I don't do outlines as much as paragraph descriptions of what it is I think I'm trying to do with the work. I believe this is crucial, to regularly articulate what my intention and hope is for the piece of writing I'm working on. This can be very revealing and helpful. I ask my writing students to do this all the time: Tell me what it is you most want the project you're working on to end up being? What are your greatest hopes for the writing?

ELIZABETH GILBERT:

I prepare hugely for each book—often preparing for years before I begin to write. The preparation usually takes the form of extensive research (reading, study, interviews, travel, observations, outlines). I need to go roll around in a world before I can write about it. I need to feel that I completely understand what I'm doing and where I'm going before I begin. I take notes on index cards, which I file tidily in shoeboxes. I've never found a better system. The more assiduously I prepare, the lighter and more joyful the actual writing experience is. I didn't understand this trick when I was a young aspiring writer; I thought you were supposed to just sit down with a blank page and create something out of thin air. Thus I suffered and twisted in empty distress. No more. Preparation is everything.

EMILY HOLLYDAY:

Lately, my process has started with writing everything that I want to say in bullet points, uncompleted sentences, and random paragraphs. I make a mess of ideas that I go back to organize into an outline. Most of the time, when I am writing a paper for school, I do a lot of research. Journal writing, however, does not require any evidence—that's why I like it.

ARUNA KENYI:

I usually have an outline! And I do research to some extent. There usually isn't much information about my country on the Internet, so I rely a lot more on my family to help on some of the issues that I want to write about regarding my country.

LILY KING:

I usually have a handful of notes, a few full sentences, not much more, before I start a novel. I do any research that is necessary as I go. My most recent novel, *Euphoria*, is the exception to all that. I had a big notebook full of notes before I started because everything about the idea was unfamiliar to me, everything I wrote about—anthropology, Papua New Guinea and its indigenous tribes, 1933—had to be researched. Once I start writing a novel, by hand in a lined notebook, I get ideas and put them in the back of the notebook. When those notes get too unruly, I create a little timeline to help me figure out where I think I'm going.

JONATHAN LETHEM:

I never outline. My preference is to keep the force of the story wanting to express itself for the telling of the story itself—I'd be afraid of spending that momentum and pressure on a provisional form like an outline. As for research, I'm usually forced to do some, just to raise my awareness of the texture and detail of some world or profession or ideology that I'm exploring—but I think it's important to do exactly as little as you feel you can get away with, in order to leave vast dark unknown areas in which your projections—your wishes, lies, and dreams—are free to take over.

ARI MEIL:

I do a huge amount of research over months when I am writing a novel, but I try to keep any outlining to a minimum. While it helps to have a sketch in my head, I find that if I write too much down, it dampens my excitement for creating on the fly. Once I have a full manuscript, I then sort the scenes into an outline and edit that so that the flow of events makes sense to me, feels right, and then I go back into the text and rewrite accordingly.

LEWIS ROBINSON:

I don't start with an outline, and I don't do research ahead of time, but once I've written about 100 pages of a novel, I'll start to outline what I've already written so that I can hold it all in my brain more easily. That's when I start to research, too.

BILL ROORBACH:

I might have a few notes on scraps of papers or my iPhone, but never from an outline, never. Outlines or similar (like index card maps), I create after several drafts are written, if ever. I do vast research and often reporting, but I start writing before I start researching so that I know what it is I really need to research. Then the research tells me what I really should be writing. And then the writing tells me what I should research. And that just keeps cycling in a big spiraling mad gyre that never ends except with publication and not even then.

GRACE WHITED:

I prefer just sit down and write with abandon, just pour whatever I'm thinking at the moment onto paper, but if I'm writing about a certain scenario or condition that I want to be accurate, I research for a couple hours. Since I prefer to write fiction, I can put my own twist on things, but if I'm writing realistic fiction I try to be as real as I can. I find the more genuine I can get, the more it touches my audience's hearts.

MISSOURI ALICE WILLIAMS:

I just write down whatever comes to mind first.

NOAH WILLIAMS:

For an idea to meet paper, or more often Microsoft Word, it has to pass three tests. First, I have to hold on to it long enough to stick in my brain so I can remember to write it down. Second, it has to be good enough to add to the running list of ideas that I keep written down. This includes the plot, the length, the venue, and what the story's all about. Finally, the story must be exciting to write. Also, I like to envision the trajectory of the time I'll be working on a piece. Is it interesting and clear enough to start writing in one sitting, or does it need a few weeks of teasing and massaging to come together? If something gets away from me, then I'll usually table it and start working on something else.

## *How much of the piece do you know before you start writing?*

CHRISTINA MURRAY:
When I write poetry, I rarely know more than the first line of what I'm going to write. That first line usually pops into my head, but what follows is never planned and never expected.

RICHARD AKERA:
I guess it depends on the topic. If I'm writing about my life, then I pretty much know most or some of the story I'm trying to tell and add to it as ideas come along. Whereas, if I'm trying to write a story about boy meets girl, I know little or nothing, but when I start to write, ideas come and I put the pieces together as I go along.

JAED COFFIN:
Sometimes, I can see the whole story/arc as clearly as I can my own two hands; other times, I have no idea at all what I'm drawn to about something, but it won't go away. But usually my story-brain is on hyperdrive, and even mundane things start shaping themselves into narratives before I can stop it from happening.

SUSAN CONLEY:
When I am writing fiction, I have very little idea of where we're going and that is the journey: heading out into the unknown of the page and letting the story unfold. The trick is to be open to the ride and to learn incredible amounts of information about characters and motives along the way. Everything is in flux in fiction. Everything can change. Nonfiction is a very different animal. The story itself is often preordained in nonfiction. We know how it starts and how it ends. So the magic of nonfiction happens in how you tell the story: how you allow for the writing to tangent and detour and tell some smaller, surprising stories within the larger, preordained story.

DAVE EGGERS:
I usually have a general sense of the overall shape of the book.

FADUMO ISSACK:
I think as a writer I don't always know the pieces I write before I start writing them down. The words that I choose to put in the writing just come to me as I write along. Whatever they are.

LILY KING:
Not much. I have more of a feeling than a plot, more of a sense of the characters and how they will affect each other than what will happen.

BILL ROORBACH:
I like this question, the way it uses the word *piece*. I know a part of a piece before I start, which is to say, not very much! But I usually start by thinking I know all.

BETSY SHOLL:
I know nothing beforehand, absolutely nothing, and am often surprised by where a poem goes. Sometimes it will take months of fiddling with images, trying one thing, then another, before I have any sense of what a poem is about. That's the part I love—not knowing, just moving images, words, voice tones around until finally they seem to have a shape, a place to go. Of course, sometimes things come together more quickly, but often it's this slow process of discovery.

GEORGE SAUNDERS:
Usually, as little as possible. That keeps a story from becoming too programmatic or preachy. My process is basically just trying to steer toward the most energetic choices—sort of like if you were piloting a raft and your job was to keep it in the rapids. And this happens sentence-to-sentence—maybe with a few broad goals (Lance will fall in love with Susan, maybe?), but also trying to stay open to what the story is trying to tell you.

GRACE WHITED:
It's funny, the way I work. Sometimes, if I'm close to the computer or a scrap of paper, I'll start writing without thinking about the entire plot. Other times, if I have no place to put my ideas, I'll continue writing inside my head until I have nearly an entire story written out in my mind. So it depends; sometimes I write from one inspiring sentence to an entire plot I worked out earlier.

NOAH WILLIAMS:
When I sit down to write, I usually have the most dramatic part of the story in my head, or else whatever scene in the story makes it interesting and exciting to write down and, hopefully, to read. Unless of course it's poetry, in which case I just go ahead and empty my head as it comes to me. I find this to be incredibly relaxing and usually pretty funny as well.

MONICA WOOD:

I know zip when I start out. I just follow my own language, sentence by sentence, until the story begins to reveal itself. That might take two years, 400 pages. Then I toss it all and begin again with what I now know. I wish there were a shortcut, but there isn't.

*Do you write chronologically from beginning to end, or craft scenes and work on transitions and placement later?*

MELISSA COLEMAN:

I tried to write the first draft of my first book chronologically, but was struggling with it until I had a dream where my deceased sister was sitting next to me stringing beads onto a necklace. She said something about just focusing on each bead, one at a time, and after that I wrote whatever memory came to me when I sat down to write. Later, during editing, I went back and ordered the resulting memory beads in time.

SUSAN CONLEY:

I tend to start at the beginning. But very quickly I jump ahead and write scenes that are calling to me. Then I go back and see where I can slot those in. It's a messy process. But I always keep that notion of the linear chronology in my head so that I can organize everything when I need to. I sort of feel like the chronological, linear arc is there so that you can disrupt it and subvert it, but it keeps on keeping on no matter what: the heartbeat that is the soundtrack of our lives.

DAVE EGGERS:

I write completely out of order, then assemble it all.

ARUNA KENYI:

No, I do not write chronologically from beginning to end. I craft scenes and work on transitions and placement later. I write down as much as I can in paragraphs randomly and then I organize it at a later time.

JONATHAN LETHEM:

My goal is to experience the text as much like a reader as possible—to feel it unfolding in front of me with the mysterious urgency I experience when I'm reading something terrific. So, that dictates always going from beginning to ending, religiously, never jumping ahead no matter how tempting. Instead, those scenes I'm so eager to write—the great set-pieces for the end of the book, usually—become spurs to production; my eagerness to get to them helps me push through the long journey.

BILL ROORBACH:
I work in a tumble that may seem chronological and sensible to me as I go, but usually turns out to be largely insane. I then fix.

MICHÉE RUNYAMBO:
At first I did try to write chronologically and it didn't work out for me, and I just decided to write scenes and put them together.

GRACE WHITED:
I used to write chronologically, but what I found is that I would be more certain about one part of the plot than the part I was working on, so I began to break apart my writing and put it together as I went on. If I can write the scenes I'm sure about first, then it can actually help me write the parts that I'm not so sure about.

MISSOURI ALICE WILLIAMS:
I have always written chronologically.

**Do you edit as you write each sentence, or edit later? How much of your writing is rewriting?**

AMIRA AL SAMMRAI:
Yes I do, because I know that nothing can be completed perfectly. Sometimes it takes me a while to edit everything as I go along, so I prefer to keep the editing until after I finish.

DAVE EGGERS:
Both. Rewriting and self-editing, and submitting to outside editing—these are key. There's something very dangerous about thinking your first drafts are so wonderful they can't be altered. If you do, you're in some serious trouble.

GIBSON FAY-LEBLANC:
I do a lot of both. I find that often my early sentences have within them the energy and tone that will help determine where I'm headed. Sometimes those

early sentences appear fairly intact, and other times I hammer them into shape and go from there. If I'm writing prose (so many words!), I tend to push myself not to edit as much as I write. I try to build momentum and then spend many hours going back and reading each sentence aloud later. If I'm writing a poem, I do tend to edit as I go (in addition to revising later), and the form and shape of the poem also help determine where I end up. However it happens, I spend a lot of time rewriting. Most of my sentences get completely rewritten.

ARUNA KENYI:

I do not edit as I write, but I edit after I have completed writing down my ideas. I normally send my writing to someone at The Telling Room to read through and get suggestions on where I can add or take information out from the writing.

ARI MEIL:

I rewrite the previous day's writing when I sit down to work each day. It refreshes my memory, gets me back in the right mindset, and makes for a tidier manuscript in the end. Today I would estimate that seventy percent of my writing is rewriting. Ask me another time and I might tell you something different.

LEWIS ROBINSON:

I've always wanted to be the kind of writer who doesn't edit while writing, but I do. I'm constantly rewriting sentences and paragraphs as I go.

BILL ROORBACH:

All of my writing is rewriting. Pretty much every word. I rewrite from my head to start, and then fix that as I go, then go back and fix everything, throwing out about half, and then rewrite some more. I do tend to make great sentences as I go along, but so many of them must be cut later anyway. Why spend the time? That's a rhetorical question, as I generally do spend the time.

RICHARD RUSSO:

As a younger writer, I never worried about revision until I'd told my story straight through to the end. Only when I knew how the narrative had resolved itself did I go back and see if I could make everything work to that end. My thinking was: Why spend a lot of time polishing a paragraph or page or chapter that I might decide to cut from the book? Now, at sixty-four, I revise constantly, at every stage of the process, partly because I hate ugly sentences and want to fix them, but also because something that's not stated precisely or clearly is a mistake that can lead to other mistakes and become part of the narrative foundation you're building on. The writing doesn't have to be perfect, but (to use a carpenter's term) it should be *plumb* (i.e., level). Out-of-kilter language makes the structure tippy. The correct word, the perfect image, the precise comparison are small truths that lead to other small truths. A good book is just a collection of these small things that ring true.

GRACE WHITED:

I find that I like to write continuously without editing, because it breaks my flow. Once I'm done with a considerable chunk, I go back and fix the flow of sentences and replace unnecessary words. But I hate rewriting because I find too many flaws in my previous writing and end up wanting to rewrite the entire story. So most of my writing is actually rough drafts.

MONICA WOOD:

Are you kidding me? All of my writing is rewriting!

# ON THE PUBLISHING PROCESS

*When is your writing finished?*

ANN BEATTIE:
When I feel I don't have to grasp at straws anymore, and they all seem just to be there: to cohere, to overlap, to be able to be held in my hand and to offer the potential of an individual moment that is suddenly potentially multi-layered with text and subtext, and to expand beyond what the scope of the story has been to that point.

MELISSA COLEMAN:
When it stops talking to me.

SARA CORBETT:
Ha, never! If I could go back and rewrite everything again, I would do it. Nothing is ever finished. It's just ripped out of your hands.

LILY KING:
I suppose when I have written many drafts, done everything I can to polish it, then have shown it to my best readers, my agent, and my editor, have taken all their advice into consideration, and rewritten it several times—then it is sort of, kind of finished. Usually, a publication date stops any further tinkering.

ARI MEIL:
I'm not someone who can rewrite forever. I feel like an overedited story begins to look like a face that's had Botox injections. It may look "prettier," but it loses the ability to express itself naturally.

MICHAEL PATERNITI:

Um . . . never? Even when I see it in print, I'm still editing in my head. Is there a diagnosis for this? Probably, but I seem to share the affliction with most writers I know.

BILL ROORBACH:

Was it Paul Valéry who said, "A poem is never finished, only abandoned"? I think so. And that's my answer, all genres.

MICHÉE RUNYAMBO:

I don't think I ever actually finish my stories. I mean, yes, I try to finish, but every time I think, Ohh, I should tell them . . .

RICHARD RUSSO:

A book (or story or essay) of mine is generally finished when I realize that further revision is actually making it worse. After that, there might be a bit more to do based on an editor's suggestions, but that falls under the heading of housekeeping.

GRACE WHITED:

My writing is finished whenever I feel like it's finished. Sometimes I might have an ending previously worked out, but as I'm coming to a conclusion I find that I like one sentence better than my prewritten sentence, so I use that instead. Most often I reread my writing and try to answer any unanswered questions that the readers might have, unless I'm going for a more open ending.

### What do titles mean to you?

AMIRA AL SAMMRAI:

Titles sometimes explain a whole story without even having to read it. A strong title should lead to an interesting story. Titles mean a lot to me. In order for me to understand a story, I first need to understand the title.

ANN BEATTIE:

I don't remember titles by other people or titles of my own work. It isn't bad memory—it's an unwillingness to isolate what has expanded throughout the work into merely yeast that made the dough rise. I do understand that you have to have a title. For years, I liked one-word titles. They seemed a sort of concession to what was expected—tentative and inherently mysterious (not enough information) and discreet. Always good to be discreet in titles, even though long, killer titles are much in vogue.

RICHARD BLANCO:
I think titles should do a lot of work for a poem. A title should be like the first line of the poem.

GIBSON FAY-LEBLANC:
Titles can do so many different kinds of work, so they're important to me, and I spend many hours on them. My book of poems probably had twenty different titles in the years I was working on it, and the novel I'm working on has had several different titles as well. Probably my fascination with titles comes from my poetic training. The title is the first thing a reader sees. It's a first line before the first line. It sets a tone. It can point into the piece or away from it. It can be an on-ramp or provide some misdirection. It can expand the meaning of a piece or narrow it. A great title can help make a good piece of writing that much better.

ARUNA KENYI:
My titles usually remind me of something or someone that's important to me. For example, the title of my memoir, *Between Two Rivers*, reminds me of my village.

JONATHAN LETHEM:
Since I never seem to be able to come up with a title that's good enough to satisfy both me and my publisher until the very last possible second, they mean that I'm finally finished!

CAMPBELL MCGRATH:
A title is like a billboard looming over the on-ramp to a highway—a great opportunity to deliver a message before the reader's journey really begins. It would be dumb just to leave that billboard blank, wouldn't it? Use your titles!

ARI MEIL:
Very little.

VASSILY MURANGIRA:

The title means a lot to me because it's what draws attention to the reader to be interested in your story. I wait to choose a title after I have finished writing. It has to fit the whole story.

BILL ROORBACH:

Titles are great. They help you know what you've written or what you're about to write, and they help transmit a layered message about the work at hand to potential readers. Kind of like perfume in a dating situation.

MICHÉE RUNYAMBO:

I think titles are the hardest to come up with. They capture an audience. It's the whole story in one little hook.

RICHARD RUSSO:

To me, titles are often revelations. A good title reveals to me that I know what my book is about. You don't have to "think it up." In one of my novels there's a restaurant called the Empire Grill. Out back of the building is a river that narrows to a falls. One day, working on the book, I mistakenly typed the word *Empire* and the word *Falls*. I stared at it for a second and realized that my subconscious had given me both the name of my town and a very layered title to my novel.

GRACE WHITED:

I value titles a lot, because the title is normally the one thing that captivates me when I'm searching for a book, other than the cover. I feel like it expresses the story in a purer, more condensed form, which is also why I don't name my stories until they are finished. Many people find that annoying about me, but it's just the way I feel is right to title my stories.

MISSOURI ALICE WILLIAMS:

A title is very important because it tells your reader what your piece is all about. I start a poem with a title and use it as a prompt. I still prefer my poem's original title, "Cigarettes."

NOAH WILLIAMS:

Titles mean everything. No one bothers to read a book with a bad title! Depending on what I'm writing, a title could be a flirtatious summary or an honest caption for an obscure piece. However, I believe that everything should have a title, and the beauty of a title is that it is forever evolving as your piece grows and changes.

MONICA WOOD:

Titles are important to me only in that once I have the title, I know what the story is about. Titles come very, very late in the process.

### How does the publisher influence your writing?

JAED COFFIN:

A lot at first, and then, when I get desperate and realize (again) that it only messes with my mind to pay attention to the publisher, I just go for it as if my contract is only with the cosmos—or something.

SARA CORBETT:

I don't think a publisher generally influences one's writing, but the best gift to a writer is to have a great editor. I've worked with the same editor for fifteen years, a brilliant, caring, and straight-shooting woman at the *New York Times Magazine* named Ilena Silverman, who has become the person for whom I write. She sets the bar for me. I think, "Will she be engaged? Will she understand what I'm saying? Will she say I'm being precious or flowery or lazy?" You know how a cat goes out hunting and leaves a dead mouse on the doorstep as an offering? I feel like I do that for my editor. I'm not going to waste her time with something insignificant or meatless. I work hard to impress her with what I lay at her feet. She's not quick to give a compliment, which means that when she does finally say you've done something well, you can be sure that you have. It's good to have someone who kicks your butt that way.

BILL ROORBACH:

In a perfect world, it's all a lovely, collaborative enterprise. But, of course, the world isn't perfect, and often sucks. But I have learned to put my foot down.

GRACE WHITED:

I'm very eager to please the greater audience, so I go along with most of what my editor and publisher say. But I do stand my ground if I don't agree with their advice. I had an experience where I was told that I should add dialogue to my writing, and although I didn't agree, I went along with it. Later I removed the dialogue from the story because I felt like it weakened the writing, and I think that was the best decision I've ever made because I was staying true to myself.

### What is the most memorable thing a reader has told you about your writing?

RICHARD AKERA:
"I was touched by your story." I will never forget that.

RICHARD BLANCO:
It's always memorable when people tell me they cried because of one of my poems.

JAED COFFIN:
"A self-indulgent journey to nowhere" was, I think, a pretty compelling summary of my first book. I think the reader gave me 1 star on Amazon. Brilliant!

ELIZABETH GILBERT:
I like it best when people tell me that they felt I was speaking directly to them, or that I had written this book directly for them. This is what I want people to feel—a sense of hushed intimacy. The fact is, I do write my books both to and for people. I have novelist friends who see it differently, who say, "I write only and entirely for myself." In a way, I understand what they're doing—they are trying to keep their creative process pure of outside influence, and trying to stay safe from the rush and disappointment of outcome, of failure and success, of other people's fickle reactions and expectations. But I see it so differently. I very much want to be in touch with the reader—whether it is to delight, to inform, to push, or to pull forth complicated emotions. I feel a responsibility when I'm writing to be aware of the reader at all times, because that's the feeling I like to have, as a reader myself, when I fall into a book. I like to feel that somebody gives a damn about who is on the other side of the page. I like the fellowship of that, the communion.

LILY KING:
When I was a sophomore in high school, my English teacher wrote at the bottom of one of my short stories: "Lily, you are the master of the family tale." I will never ever forget that or the feeling it gave me, and still gives me, decades later.

CHRISTINA MURRAY:
I was once told that my poetry tends to come off as sarcastic, funny, and out-going—something that is unexpected from a shy and reserved person such as myself.

LEWIS ROBINSON:
After my first book was published, I happened to go back to my old high school and saw some of my old teachers. One of them said, "I read the book. I feel like you took this town, cut it up into little pieces, put those pieces in a bag, and shook it all up." I knew the book bothered her, and I felt bad. But now when I think about that conversation, I feel kind of giddy.

BILL ROORBACH:
I wrote about a dead friend, and his mom said my writing brings him back to life for her every year on his birthday.

RICHARD RUSSO:
Occasionally I'll be on book tour or giving a talk somewhere, and someone will come up to me and say that a book of mine got them through a round of chemotherapy or helped them deal with some terrible loss. One man told me that after reading my novel *The Risk Pool* he put the book down and called his father, to whom he hadn't spoken in thirty years. Why do we read? Why do we write? That's why.

GRACE WHITED:
I recall that someone once told me they looked up to me and wished to write like me in the future, which thrilled me because I have spent most of my life looking up to others, so being a role model to another person really motivated me. Many people also come up to me and tell me that my writing touches them and almost brings them to tears, which tells me that I can be and am influential to others. The first time someone other than my family or friend asked me for an autograph, I was blown away because I realized my writing was valued, and that I wasn't so far away from my dream of being an author after all.

MISSOURI ALICE WILLIAMS:
People have always told me they like my writing because it has "a voice."

MONICA WOOD:
A woman from Oregon once wrote to me to say that she read one of my novels aloud to her mother after her father's death, and it healed a rift they'd been suffering for twenty-five years. I cried my eyes out.

*Of the people you know, who do you most hope enjoys reading this book?*

RICHARD AKERA:
Of all the people that I know, I hope Elvis enjoys reading this book the most. This piece is for Elvis, my little brother.

ANN BEATTIE:
I hope someone is surprised by the concept of the book and that it makes the process of writing seem as interesting and as interactive as it really is.

JAED COFFIN:
My mother and, soon enough, my daughters.

MELISSA COLEMAN:
All young writers, my own daughters included!

EMILY HOLLYDAY:
I hope seniors enjoy reading this book because they have so many stories to share. Perhaps these pieces will spark their memories.

FADUMO ISSACK:
Of the people I know, I hope one day my son enjoys reading this book. Also my family and friends. Teachers and mentors.

LILY KING:
I hope it's someone who has always wanted to write but has maybe never even known it or admitted it and this person reads these pieces, and suddenly it is all clear and the desire emerges fully formed because it has always been there waiting for this moment.

JULIAN MAYORQUIN:
My marketing team, the people I work together with.

CAMPBELL MCGRATH:

I hope that my kids enjoy this book—the stories it offers, of young lives and hardships endured, and the message about literature as a means of negotiating those difficulties are really great lessons. I plan to give this book to my own kids and my nephews.

MICHAEL PATERNITI:

My daughter May! She's going to love this book because she's always writing stories in response to what she reads. Her room is littered with journals and scraps of paper, full of notes and sketches. For her, each story is its own journey. She buckles her belt, looks out the window, and then lets the words carry her away. I think this book is going be an overnight flight to somewhere really cool for her.

BILL ROORBACH:

Each of its readers, one at a time, even those I don't know.

GRACE WHITED:

I hope that people aspiring to be authors in the future will be motivated by this book, because just a year ago I had never been published and now here I am, preparing to be in my second Telling Room anthology. Your dreams are never far from reach, as long as you keep heading toward them.

MISSOURI ALICE WILLIAMS:

Personally, I hope all my friends and family enjoy reading the book, but most importantly, all the authors and poets out there.

# WRITING PROMPTS

### Hyenas/Cheekbone

In "Hyenas" and "Cheekbones," Mohamed and Gilbert use two different forces to create a powerful story. Mohamed shapes reality around the family voice and form, while Gilbert measures gravity in zygomatic arches and hearts. How do you create power in a storyline? Write a story that uses a consistent skeleton for "power."

### Breathing in the Rain/Burning in the Rain

In poetry, words sit in place on the page to lift off into more than one meaning. Al Sammrai and Blanco use the form to mirror the effect of the rain. Al Sammrai plays with line lengths with clean slippery language that drop into each other, while Blanco uses language and structure that connote rain-soaked, sopping heavy verse. Choose an experience that is shaped by environment. Write a poem that actively uses the structure to mirror meaning.

### Carrots/Carrot Spotting

How do you create mood through writing? What is the mood of these two pieces? How do you know?

In "Carrots" Murray writes, "If I had been a carrot, I know I would have been normal." Write about a part of yourself you wish you could change, or write about a part of yourself you know you wouldn't change. Why and how?

Lethem writes, "I always knew the vegetables had arrived at their identities for some special reason, out of some special need." Write about a time you witnessed someone change "for some special reason, out of some special need."

### Wildernesses/Heat Rises

"Wildernesses" and "Heat Rises" bounce off each other and reverberate with new meanings taken from counterparts that the two represent. Choose a piece of writing, 500 words or less, that calls you to want to mirror particular styles, ideas, or even characters.

### *The Fate of the Trees/That Leafless Tree*

"We were the only ones / to worry about / the fate of the trees." Fate is both a personal dream and nagging obligation. Write about an experience with "fate."

"It asked in a scratchy voice, or I heard / Then wordless went out to feel how other / it was, how real, that guardian, elder / sentry at my window, that leafless tree." Both Nasrat's and Sholl's poems deal with the experience of feeling responsible for or yearning to be connected to the fate of someone / something beyond themselves. Write about a time you felt alone and sought connection.

### *A Day in Three Worlds/Night and Day*

It is human nature to try to categorize life. In "A Day in Three Worlds," Jeylani writes about the struggle to balance his identity in all three worlds—Somalia, Nairobi, and America, but also school, basketball, and religion. In "Night and Day," McGrath accepts duality in both structure (prose and poetry) and content: "Fasting and feasting, developed and undeveloped, spiritual and secular, past and present—so many dualities, these binary pairings we utilize to organize and explain the world and our lived experiences." If you had to write your life into categories, how would you go about it? Where are things not so clearly divisible?

In "A Day in Three Worlds," Jeylani writes, "I've gained all these things, but I've lost something and I want to recover it." Write about a time you lost something—a physical object or a feeling. Did you recover it? How?

Sometimes, not saying anything can be more powerful than saying something. At the Y, Mustaf and Omar are not wearing the right clothes for playing basketball. Jeylani writes: "What I don't say is that I remember when I was like that, not knowing what to wear, not being used to having so many different kinds of clothes to choose from." Write a list of sentences that begin with, "What I don't say . . ." Choose one and write about the effect of not saying anything in that moment.

### *Bottle Jacking/Go to Jail, After Eight Times, Go Directly to Jail*

Mayorquin writes about processing Gale's actions: "This kid was my best friend. And all this started by smoking a couple of bowls before catching the bus to Lincoln Middle School. And I introduced him to it." Write about a time you felt you had an impact on someone that was greater (for better or worse) than you expected.

In "Go to Jail," Saunders deals with his distance from his characters: "My relation to this Mexican kid, then, is something like that of a plumber's apprentice to a leak." Write about a time you unexpectedly related to someone who was different.

Write about a time you had to learn to unrelate to someone you were once close with. Did it happen quickly, or over time as it does in "Bottle Jacking?"

### I Started to Explain/Drinking Water

"I could tell that she was hurting, and it always bothered me to see her go through all of the pain alone. I felt horrible about myself, that I couldn't do anything to help her out, but just sit back and witness her bleed from the inside." Write about a time you felt helpless.

Write a script for a scene from one of your favorite books. How do you incorporate internal dialogue? Does it become external dialogue or converge into physical behavior?

### Swimming to Safety/Drive-by Alligator

In "Swimming to Safety" and "Drive-by Alligator," story plays an important part in dealing with tragedy. As things change around the main characters, the story itself becomes a way to hold on to things as they were before life changed. Write about a story, either one you have read or one that is from personal experience, that helps you cope with challenging times.

Both Murangira and Beattie comment on the purpose behind storytelling. Murangira writes, "But this is not the story I want to tell because it reminds me of many unbearable memories. Instead, I will tell you about a time in Africa that makes me smile." While Beattie writes, "No, people would say, don't know that duo, but even if they existed, what is the *meaning* of the story of the alligator in Florida for everyone else, how does its larger significance waft off like a white cloud in a blue sky to make an intriguing Rorschach blot whose interpretation will of course never be wrong and never be right?"

Write an essay that answers one or both of the following questions: Why do we tell stories? Whom do we tell stories for?

### A Sandwich *and* An Olive/Jammy Brightness

Practice pulling writing apart and putting it back together again. For example, Meil picks parts of Mathieson's poetry:

At the bottom my grubby hands
reach into the roots & pull up the dirt
& move inside the tree,
a strong tree, a living tree,
a body branching into our community,
an apple tree, a taste I remember.

When I am there
I imagine a little apartment
in the center of time
where my summer has just begun.

He weaves it into his own prose, making the language come to life in a different way:

Surrounded by earth with nothing on my mind but eating one of the huge sandwiches my uncle always makes me when I return home to my one happy tree, I crawl desperately through the soil, digging my way in the darkness until I feel it: a root that has reached down through space, through the various levels of reality and dreams, through time itself to guide me back to the center. And once I've felt it I know that I am on my way back home. I pull my hands through the dirt, guided by the loving curves of that ever-twining, powerful-reaching tendril until I emerge at the base of the tree. The tree at the center of time. My home.

Choose a piece of poetry and write it into prose, or choose a piece of prose and assemble it into poetry.

### The Table/The Table

As Hilowle highlights, some things such as names are selectively and inherently imbued with meaning. Other concrete, seemingly universal objects are reborn with fresh meaning in a new context. While both Hilowle and Conley write about the table, each writer highlights how singularly important *that* table was in its environment. Write about an object that is alive with your unique family personality.

### The Bump/Summer

Life was simple before motherhood bumped into me.

\* \* \*

I want to say it was a mistake getting pregnant but it wasn't.

\* \* \*

... she presses her lips to the top of her baby's head, the soft part that's dented in a bit like a bruise on a peach as if that kid were cute and sound asleep as if she were deaf to the hollering and numb to the kicking as if that baby would never do wrong no matter how many mistakes.

These are examples of lines that contain an element of surprise—note, for each, what is surprising, and then work to emulate that element of surprise in a few lines of your own.

### Hunting in the Deep Woods/When Dad Rode Past Me

First impressions can do a lot. Williams uses first impressions of outerwear to distinguish between the toughness of two characters: "I look at his fancy glasses, immaculate blaze-orange parka with a black camouflage print, the glittering rifle in his hand, and then back to my beat up old 30-30 and I think of the two pairs of pants I'm wearing." Robinson also uses outerwear to highlight how out of place he feels when he writes: "That's when I'd wanted to explain to him: we'd never worn Lycra shorts before. I wanted to take off our bike helmets, our bike jerseys, and show the guy we were regular people." Write a scene in which two characters meet; describe their relationship using language that only pertains to first appearances.

Both Williams and Robinson write about an experience that made the main character grateful for what he already had. Write about a new experience that made you appreciate something you already had.

### Two Teeth/History Lesson

Families are made up of piles of memories of small moments. Write about one of these memories, teasing out the unspeakable greatness through a small moment. How has your family grown from that foundational memory?

### Cantaloupe/Self-Portrait, with Dish Rag

Both Fay-LeBlanc and Hollyday write about using boots, magic, and tintinnabulations to make life stick together. Write about what makes your life stick together.

Fay-LeBlanc and Hollyday use the repetition of the word *tintinnabulations,* which is an example of onomatopoeia, a literary device in which the word evokes the sound it describes to add an auditory dimension to their poems. Write a list of words that are onomatopoeic, and write a poem that uses your favorite one.

These poems are sestinas. Research the form of the sestina, and write your own.

### A Little Secret/Goddess of Liberation

Both Williams and Coleman write about not being enough for boys to look at, in contrast to other female acquaintances. Williams writes: "Whenever she would take her leather jacket off / all you would see / were these huge things / and all the boys would go, / 'Yahoo.'" Coleman opens her story; "I wish I could be like Tara. She has super thick long black hair, olive skin, round dark eyes, and is starting to get boobs. I have short hair, a million freckles, and a flat chest." Write about a time when you felt you needed to change to feel accepted or noticed.

Coleman and Williams create distance from the experience of being a woman by alienating it or making it foreign, to shed new light on the experience. Williams writes about breasts as "these huge things" that made all the boys go "'Yahoo,'" while Coleman writes about being feminine from the point of view of cows who "were pitifully female, with their ungainly udders and slow eyes." Write about a part of yourself from an alien perspective. What language do you use? How do you explain its importance or usefulness?

### Climbing Barefoot/The Coconut Tree

In "Climbing Barefoot," Issack writes "Pain became my friend . . . the best thing about it was that it let me know that I was alive." In "The Coconut Tree," Coffin writes about slicing his foot and being healed by his grandfather as a strong and important memory. Write about a time when pain showed you something surprising.

Both Issack and Coffin write about symbols; Issack writes about scars on the outside representing something on the inside, and Coffin writes about memory as "symbolic, somehow, for something you need to understand at the time." Write about a memory, a scar, a person that is symbolic for something you became, learned, or shared.

### Box of Hope/Pull the Sled, Feed the Fire

Whited and Eggers write narratives that intentionally omit names for the characters, creating a specific tone for each piece. Write a narrative without using proper nouns. How does this influence the tone of your writing? These pieces have been referred to as fables. What makes them so, aside from the omitted names?

In "Pull the Sled, Feed the Fire," Eggers writes about feeding the fire: "The work of keeping it strong is simple and feels good. The best work is work you know is necessary, is within your ability, and will end." Write about your own kind of work that "you know is necessary, is within your ability, and will end."

In both "Box of Hope" and "Pull the Sled, Feed the Fire," a universal symbol is uniquely treasured by the one who comes into possession of it. Write about the transformation of an object into a treasure. How does an object turn into a treasure?

### The Faithful Doves of My Father/I Thought I Could Fix Things

Moments of great sorrow can sometimes feel as if they were predestined; something or someone was different, there was a warning sign unnoticed. You spend time thinking about the moment in reverse slow motion. Write about a time of loss or grief in reverse. Were there signs?

Although Sharafyar and Corbett experience great sorrow at the loss of a parent, each frames the story in hope. Sharafyar writes of her hopes for a career, for a return home, to be just like her father. Corbett writes, "Because really you have no choice but to acknowledge pain and then keep living. Defiantly, stupidly, hopefully, compassionately." Write about a time you held on to hope in a time of great pain.

Write a response to the statement: "I understand now that life is full of small rehearsals."

### The Photograph/We Are Trying to Understand What Happened to You There

Through story, Paterniti and Kenyi write that memories come to life. Write from a memory you wish you could bring back to life.

Both Kenyi and Paterniti write about telling a story through pictures, "so that others might see." Select three photographs. What do they help you see or show others? What story do the three pictures shape together?

In "We Are Trying to Understand What Happened to You There," Paterniti writes: "In a perfect world, this is how it should work: you speak—and we listen, as if it happened to us."

Write a series of statements that begin, "In a perfect world, this is how it should work . . ." Choose one, and write a poem, essay, or narrative responding to that statement.

# THE CONTRIBUTORS

RICHARD AKERA is a writer at The Telling Room. He is published in two anthologies, *Illumination* and *Exit 13*, and a film, *The Whole World Waiting*. He was a finalist in the 2014 Maine Literary Awards for "Dog," which is a true story and takes place in Kampala, Uganda. Richard, known as AK, is also a dance teacher and a performer. During his free time, AK volunteers at the YMCA of Southern Maine and enjoys reading, running, and spending time with his family and friends.

AMIRA AL SAMMRAI is from Iraq and is twenty years old. She has lived in the United States since running from death and killing in Iraq in 2009. Her poem "Breathing in the Rain" was published in The Telling Room's anthology *Exit 13* and came out of the writing she did in the Young Writers & Leaders program. Al Sammrai graduated from high school in 2012. She's married and is now in her first year of college.

ANN BEATTIE lives in Maine and in Charlottesville, Virginia. Her husband, Lincoln Perry, is a painter. Her writing has been translated into many languages, including book publications in France, Italy, Holland, Germany, Sweden, Spain, Japan, etc. "The New Yorker Stories" will be published in France, Spain, Portugal, and China, and is still on submission elsewhere. An interview with Beattie has appeared in the *Paris Review*, issue 196.

RICHARD BLANCO was chosen as the fifth U.S. inaugural poet in 2013. He is the author of three collections of poems, including *Directions to the Beach of the Dead*, winner of the PEN American Beyond Margins Award and *Looking for the Gulf Motel*, winner of the 2013 Maine Literary Award for Poetry. His poems have appeared in numerous publications, including *The Best American Poetry* and *Ploughshares*.

JAED COFFIN's first book, *A Chant to Soothe Wild Elephants*, chronicles the summer he spent as a monk in his mother's village in Thailand. His next book, *Roughhouse Friday*, is about the year he won the middleweight title of a barroom boxing show. Coffin lives in Brunswick, his hometown, with his wife and two daughters, and around the corner from his mother and sister, in the neighborhood where he grew up.

MELISSA COLEMAN's memoir, *This Life Is in Your Hands: One Dream, Sixty Acres, and a Family's Heartbreak*, was a *New York Times* bestseller and a finalist for the New England Book Award. She and her husband are raising their twin girls in Maine, where the winters may be long but the kids learn to be strong.

SUSAN CONLEY's novel, *Paris Was the Place*, was published in 2013. Her memoir, *The Foremost Good Fortune*, won the Maine Literary Award for Memoir in 2011. Other work has appeared in the *New York Times Magazine*, the *Paris Review*, the *New York Times*, *Ploughshares*, and elsewhere. Susan Conley is a founder of The Telling Room and lives in Portland with her husband and two boys.

SARA CORBETT is a contributing writer at the *New York Times Magazine* and one of The Telling Room's founders. She coauthored *A House in the Sky*, which was named one of Amazon's top ten books of 2013. She hasn't owned a cat since childhood.

DAVE EGGERS is the author of nine books, including most recently *The Circle* and *A Hologram for the King*, which was a finalist for the 2012 National Book Award. Eggers is the cofounder of 826 National, a network of eight tutoring centers around the country, and ScholarMatch, a nonprofit organization designed to connect students with resources, schools, and donors to make college possible. He lives in Northern California with his family.

GIBSON FAY-LEBLANC's first collection of poems, *Death of a Ventriloquist*, was chosen by Lisa Russ Spaar for the Vassar Miller Prize and published in 2012. He lives with his family in Portland, Maine, where he can be found some nights scrubbing cantaloupe off the table and floor.

ELIZABETH GILBERT is the author of six works of fiction and nonfiction, including *Eat, Pray, Love* and *The Signature of All Things*. When she can't be found in New Jersey, she can be found on an airplane, trying to go to as many places as possible, and all at the same time.

MAHAD HILOWLE is the author of "The Table," which is the closing narrative essay in *Tearing Down the Playground*. He won the inaugural Founder's Prize, an annual award that is given to the author of the best piece of writing to come out of a Telling Room program. It is fitting that Susan Conley, one of the founders, gets to appear opposite Hilowle in their paired essays in this collection.

EMILY PLUM HOLLYDAY was inspired to write "Cantaloupe" while sitting in the grass at Turkey Hill Farm. She finished the poem that night leaning over her kitchen counter. It was published in The Telling Room's 2010 anthology *Can I Call You Cheesecake?* Since then, her heart has been in food and farming. At College of the Atlantic, in Bar Harbor, Maine, Hollyday focuses on food systems and science education through her study of human ecology.

FADUMO ISSACK loves to write. This was her first published piece, and it appeared as the title piece in The Telling Room's 2011 book *How to Climb Trees* and garnered her the prestigious Founder's Prize. She hopes to publish more, and more often. She was born in a large refugee camp east of Kenya. She came to the United States when she was twelve years old. She now lives in Portland, Maine, with her family and is the first college graduate in her extended Somali family. She hopes to be a nurse.

HASSAN JEYLANI comes from a multitalented family. His brother and sister write alongside him and their poetry and narrative accompany his story in The Telling Room's first anthology, *I Remember Warm Rain*, published in 2007. We hadn't heard from Jeylani for several years until he popped in at our writing studio a few months ago. "I'm back," he said in the doorway. "Get ready to see much more of me!"

When ARUNA KENYI was seventeen and a student at Portland High, he wrote a story called "The Photograph" with The Telling Room's cofounder Michael Paterniti, which appeared in *I Remember Warm Rain*. In 2010, he published a memoir, *Between Two Rivers*, which is being reprinted in 2014. Sales of

Kenyi's memoir helped him pay for college and supported the Sudanese Lunch Program, which he founded. Since its successful launch, instability in South Sudan has made it impossible for him to return.

LILY KING is the author of four novels, *The Pleasing Hour*, *The English Teacher*, *Father of the Rain*, and *Euphoria*. King has volunteered at The Telling Room since its beginning. She thinks it is the coolest place ever. She lives with her husband and children in Yarmouth, Maine.

JONATHAN LETHEM is the author of nine novels, including *Dissident Gardens* and *The Fortress of Solitude*. His fifth, *Motherless Brooklyn*, won the National Book Critic's Circle Award. His stories and essays have appeared in the *New Yorker*, *Harper's*, *Rolling Stone*, and many other publications.

We first found JANET MATHIESON in a field, wearing overalls and a hoodie. Her words were tiny bits of scrawl at many angles on a spare piece of paper. She didn't want to share them. Somehow, we wrested them from her and patched them together, and in the end, she stood in a circle in the field with her peers and read her words for all to hear. Today Mathieson is a student at Pitzer College, and her poems can also be found in *Can I Call You Cheesecake?*

JULIAN MAYORQUIN didn't know he was a writer, but definitely had a story he wanted to tell. The title of this book comes from that story, which he first told to his Telling Room writing coach in the hallway of his public school's alternative education classroom, and which was later published in the anthology *Tearing Down the Playground*. Now Mayorquin's a suit-and-tie kind of a guy living a glorious and sober life in Boston.

CAMPBELL MCGRATH is the author of ten books of poetry, most recently *In the Kingdom of the Sea Monkeys* (Ecco Press, 2012). He lives in Miami Beach with his wife and, on occasion, his children, who bother to visit from time to time.

People keep telling ARI MEIL that his writing is "really imaginative," and he's never quite sure if it is meant as a compliment. Also, he is beginning to think his obsession with Japanese noir manga from the '70s is not cool, just weird. Meil lives in Rockport, Maine, with his family, spotty cell coverage, and a creek running through the backyard.

ALI MOHAMED is known by some as "Hyena Killer." His story is still celebrated at his alma mater, Portland High School, where recently a classroom full of kids read it aloud and clapped loudly after a hush and the memorialized last line, "And I've got nothing left to prove." We swear we saw Mohamed grow taller even as he wrote his story with his mentor and published it in The Telling Room's book *I Remember Warm Rain* in 2007. He now makes his home in the great state of Texas.

VASSILY MURANGIRA was born in Burundi and lives in South Portland, Maine. His writing is featured in The Telling Room's book *How to Climb Trees*. He is majoring in chemical engineering at the University of Maine. Besides writing, Murangira enjoys playing sports, listening to music, and spending time with friends.

CHRISTINA MURRAY lives in Portland, Maine, and attends Smith College in Massachusetts, where she has grown as a writer since she wrote "Carrots" for the anthology *Can I Call You Cheesecake?* and has come especially to identify as a poet. She has had poems published in *Voices and Visions*, an online journal for students who attend women's colleges, and is now the editor-in-chief of the magazine.

ELIAS NASRAT was a two-year student in The Telling Room's Young Writers & Leaders program. He is a natural poet and nonfiction writer. One of his essays appears in *Exit 13*, and he also stars in the film *The Whole World Waiting*. Nasrat is originally from Afghanistan and is currently a student at the University of Maine in Orono.

MICHAEL PATERNITI is a writer living in Portland, Maine. He is a co-founder of The Telling Room and wrote a book by the same name. He still dreams of being a lion tamer.

LEWIS ROBINSON is the author of the novel *Water Dogs* and the story collection *Officer Friendly and Other Stories*. His short fiction and essays have appeared in *Sports Illustrated*, *Tin House*, the *Missouri Review*, the *New York Times Book Review*, and on NPR's program *Selected Shorts*. His dream to play in the NBA is still alive.

BILL ROORBACH's latest novel, the bestseller *Life Among Giants*, is in development with HBO as a drama series. His next novel, *The Remedy for Love*, is due in October 2014. His award-winning book of stories, *Big Bend*, has just been reissued by University of Georgia Press. His memoir in nature, *Temple Stream*, is coming soon in a new edition from Down East Books. Bill lives in Farmington, Maine, where he stands in the garden all summer and daydreams.

MICHÉE RUNYAMBO was born in May 1994 in the Republic of Congo. He spent fourteen years in Rwanda and then moved to the U.S. in 2009. He joined The Telling Room in 2012. He has written many short stories, and a few of them were published in The Telling Room's anthologies *Illumination* and *Exit 13* and in the film *The Whole World Waiting*. He was a finalist in the 2014 Maine Literary Awards for "Two Teeth."

Award-winning novelist and screenwriter RICHARD RUSSO is the author of seven novels and two short story collections. *Empire Falls* won the Pulitzer Prize for fiction in 2002. His most recent book is the memoir *Elsewhere*. He lives with his wife in Portland, Maine.

GEORGE SAUNDERS teaches writing at Syracuse University. His most recent book, *Tenth of December*, was a finalist for the National Book Award, the Story Prize, and the Folio Prize.

DARCIE SERFES began her poem when she was still a student in high school and was pregnant with her daughter. She returned to writing again after Madison's birth, and the poem was published in *Tearing Down the Playground* in 2009. Madison is now five years old, and Darcie is hoping to return to writing after her second child arrives. She has so much more to say and write about.

AQILA SHARAFYAR was a junior in high school when she first told the story about the doves her father once kept in Afghanistan. She was one of fifteen students who hailed from countries in the Middle East and eastern Africa and had found their way to Portland, Maine, and chose to tell their stories in *I Remember Warm Rain*.

COLIN SHEPARD wrote "Wildernesses" while at Casco Bay High School. It anchors the 2008 anthology *I Carry It Everywhere: 50 Teenagers on What*

*Really Matters*. In the book, Shepard stands for a photographer and brandishes a poster board, on which he has written in large black letters in all caps: "When I say freedom, I mean the freedom to do what you love," which is advice he still lives by every day.

BETSY SHOLL's eighth collection of poems, *Otherwise Unseeable*, was just published by the University of Wisconsin Press, winner of its Four Lakes Poetry Prize. She teaches in the MFA Program of Vermont College of Fine Arts and lives in Portland with her husband, not far from her two children and their families. She was Maine Poet Laureate from 2006 to 2011.

GRACE WHITED wrote "The Box of Hope," a short story that won The Telling Room's Founder's Prize in 2013 and was published in the anthology *Illumination*. She lives in South Portland, Maine, with her mother and seven cats, and attends high school as a freshman. You can often find her at home writing poems and stories on the back of her unfinished homework.

MISSOURI ALICE WILLIAMS's poem "Aida" was selected by former Maine Poet Laureate Wes McNair as a finalist at the Merriconeag Poetry Festival 2011. Her poem "A Little Secret" first appeared in The Telling Room's book *How to Climb Trees*. Since then, Missouri Alice has been quietly writing poems and plays and pursuing the theatre when not chasing small children as part of her college studies in childhood development.

NOAH WILLIAMS was first published by The Telling Room in the anthology *Exit 13*, and he was a 2013 Maine Literary Award finalist for his piece "Just Cold Enough for Comfort." He is a Young Emerging Author fellow with The Telling Room, where he is finishing his book *Hemingway's Ghost*, and lives in Portland, Maine.

MONICA WOOD is the bestselling author of the memoir *When We Were the Kennedys* and the novels *Any Bitter Thing*, *Ernie's Ark*, *My Only Story*, and *Secret Language*. She also writes books for writers and teachers. Her nonfiction has appeared in *Oprah*, the *New York Times*, *Martha Stewart Living*, *Parade*, and many other publications. Her first play, *Papermaker*, will be produced in 2015 at Portland Stage. She lives in Portland with her husband and a portly, toothless, geriatric cat named Minnie.

# ACKNOWLEDGMENTS

Our foremost thanks go to the authors in this book: The young writers and their families and supporters, including their parents and teachers; and the adults who donated their time and words to make this project such a success. A special thanks to Ann Beattie for being the very first to contribute a matching piece and incite the rest into joining in the fun.

Thank you to an incredible editorial crew who met regularly on the project over many months at The Telling Room: Molly McGrath, Gibson Fay-LeBlanc, Abigail Chance, and David Caron. They selected the pieces, made the magical pairings, and shaped the book in countless other ways. Thanks to Rose Heithoff, Erin Barnett, Andrew Griswold, Patty Hagge, Joe Conway, Molly Haley, Nick Schuller, and Sonya Tomlinson for extra editorial support and constant enthusiasm. Special gratitude to Heather Davis and Celine Kuhn at The Telling Room for being huge backers in such an undertaking.

Thanks, too, to the rest of the cast of characters who make the play with words happen on a daily basis at The Telling Room, year after year: The incomparable staff, board, teaching artists, interns, and volunteers who make what we do so great.

Great thanks to Ari Meil for hatching the idea with Molly McGrath in a Camden coffee shop way back when: High five, Ari man—we did it! Thank you to Lincoln Paine and Genevieve Morgan for their delightful editorial conversation and consultation; to Sean Wilkinson and the team at Might & Main for their stylish and smart cover design; and to Janet Robbins of North Wind Design & Production for her equally stylish text design. Thanks to David Meiklejohn for conceptualizing the book as a film trailer. And thank you to Tris Coburn and Jon Eaton at Tilbury House for believing in the book from the get-go, and to rest of the incredible bunch at Tilbury House for helping to make it happen.

Last, thank you to Susan Conley, Sara Corbett, and Mike Paterniti. These three gifted writers founded The Telling Room. They deserve all the credit in the world for seeing that every kid has a story to tell and for making it possible for them to share those stories with us all.

# ABOUT THE TELLING ROOM

The Telling Room is a nonprofit writing center in Portland, Maine, dedicated to the idea that children and young adults are natural storytellers. Focused on young writers of ages 6 to 18, we seek to build confidence, strengthen literacy skills, and provide audiences for our students' stories. We believe that the power of creative expression can change our communities and prepare our youth for future success.

Our fun, innovative programs enlist the support of local writers, artists, teachers, and community groups. We offer free afterschool workshops and tutoring at our downtown writing center, and we host field trips for school groups from all over Maine. We also lead workshops at local schools and community organizations; bring acclaimed writers to Maine to give public readings and work with small groups of students; publish bestselling anthologies of student work and books like this one by our young authors; and carry out community-wide storytelling projects and events.

We serve those who are reluctant to write as well as those who already identify as writers, including: children and young adults who are a part of Maine's growing community of immigrants and refugees, those with emotional and behavioral challenges, students struggling in mainstream classrooms, homeschoolers enthusiastic to join a creative community, and passionate young writers who need additional support beyond what their schools are able to provide. To learn more, please check us out online.

*www.tellingroom.org*

# TELLING ROOM BOOKS

The Telling Room prints, promotes, and distributes books of stories, poems, and personal narratives by the young writers who work with us in our writing programs. These professionally edited and beautifully designed books are made in-house with the help of our students and are printed locally. The Telling Room produces between ten and fifteen titles a year, and since the publication of *I Remember Warm Rain* in 2007, we have published thousands of young authors in nearly fifty books, including:

### Student Anthologies

*Beyond the Picket Fence*
*Illumination*
*Exit 13*
*How to Climb Trees*
*Can I Call You Cheesecake?*
*Tearing Down the Playground*
*I Carry It Everywhere*
*I Remember Warm Rain*

### Featured Works

*Forced* by Zahro Hassan
*Sleeping Through Thunder* by Grace Roberts
*The Road to Terrencefield* by Henry Spritz
*Hemingway's Ghost* by Noah Williams
*Between Two Rivers* by Aruna Kenyi
*Fufu and Fresh Strawberries*
by Caitlin Lowell and Charlotte McDonald

Find these books at:
**tellingroom.org/store**

All proceeds from the sale of Telling Room books
support our free writing programs for Maine youth.